Controlling und Rechnungslegung – Managerial and Financial Accounting

Series Editor

Maik Lachmann, Lehrstuhl für Controlling und Rechnungslegung, TU Berlin, Berlin, Germany

In dieser Reihe werden aktuelle Forschungserkenntnisse im Bereich Controlling und Rechnungslegung publiziert. Methodisch liegt der Schwerpunkt auf empirischen und experimentellen Studien, die den Erkenntnisstand für Wissenschaft und Praxis erweitern und vertiefen. Forschungsarbeiten, die in dieser Reihe veröffentlicht werden, nehmen eine innovative Sichtweise auf aktuelle Themenstellungen im Bereich Controlling oder Rechnungslegung ein und generieren auf Basis anspruchsvoller Forschungsmethoden neuartige wissenschaftliche Erkenntnisse. Ein Fokus wird dabei auf verhaltensorientierte Aspekte von Controlling und Rechnungslegung gelegt.

This series aims to provide an outlet for recent research in the areas of managerial and financial accounting. It includes empirical and experimental studies that contribute to a deeper understanding of accounting theory and practice. Research published in this series takes an innovative view on current topics in managerial and financial accounting to provide novel insights based on rigorous research design. A focus of this series are behavioral aspects of managerial and financial accounting.

More information about this series at http://www.springer.com/series/16139

Oliver Holtkemper

Digitization of the Management Accounting Function

A Case Study Analysis on Manufacturing Companies

Springer Gabler

Oliver Holtkemper
Coesfeld, Germany

Berlin, Technische Universität, Diss., 2020

ISSN 2524-5686 ISSN 2524-5694 (electronic)
Controlling und Rechnungslegung – Managerial and Financial Accounting
ISBN 978-3-658-31508-5 ISBN 978-3-658-31509-2 (eBook)
https://doi.org/10.1007/978-3-658-31509-2

Responsible Editor: Carina Reibold
This Springer Gabler imprint is published by the registered company Springer Fachmedien Wiesbaden GmbH part of Springer Nature.
The registered company address is: Abraham-Lincoln-Str. 46, 65189 Wiesbaden, Germany

Abstract

This study analyzes the impact of digitization on management accounting in five manufacturing companies. It is one of the first in-depth empirical studies on the intersection of management accounting and digitization. Whereas previous studies focus on a broader set of functions (e.g., finance and accounting) or a single type of characteristic of management accounting, here, the author analyzes the overall impact of digitization on the management accounting function. Interviews were conducted with stakeholders from different roles and with varying perspectives on the management accounting function within each of the five companies. Additionally, interviews with experts on specific aspects of digitization of the management accounting function were conducted.

This study suggests that there are two archetypes of change models regarding the digitization of the management accounting function. The first archetype emphasizes top-down-driven changes that aim to enhance efficiency, such as conducting tasks with a higher degree of automation in a leaner structure with fewer (human) resources. The second archetype is strongly driven and initiated by employees in the management accounting function (bottom-up). Here, the focus is on improving the use of data by applying innovative analytics methods, integrating additional sources of data, and benefiting from new technologies like artificial intelligence. Out of the five companies studied, three are focusing on bottom-up changes, one applies a top-down approach to improve efficiency in the management accounting function, and the last company does not focus on either but demonstrates characteristics of both archetypes.

Additionally, the results indicate that the digitization of the management accounting function is mostly in line with the overall company strategy. On the one hand, in a phase of cost-reduction, management accounting is treated as any other function in which processes are automated and costs are reduced where possible. On the other hand, it is treated as a beneficial supporter of strategic and operative decision-making in a company growth phase.

Zusammenfassung

Diese Studie analysiert die Auswirkungen der Digitalisierung auf das Management Accounting in fünf produzierenden Unternehmen. Sie ist eine der ersten vertieften empirischen Studien an der Schnittstelle von Management Accounting und Digitalisierung. Während sich die bisherigen Studien auf eine breitere Funktionspalette (z. B. gesamtes Finanz- und Rechnungswesen) oder eine einzelne Ausprägung des Management Accounting konzentrieren, analysiert der Autor hier den Gesamteinfluss der Digitalisierung auf das Management Accounting. Es wurden Interviews mit Stakeholdern aus unterschiedlichen Rollen und mit unterschiedlichen Perspektiven auf das Management Accounting in den fünf Unternehmen durchgeführt. Zusätzlich wurden Interviews mit Experten zu spezifischen Aspekten der Digitalisierung des Management Accountings durchgeführt.

Diese Studie legt nahe, dass es zwei Archetypen von Veränderungsmodellen bezüglich der Digitalisierung des Management Accountings gibt. Der erste Archetyp betont top-down getriebene Veränderungen, die auf Effizienzsteigerung abzielen, wie z. B. die Durchführung von Aufgaben mit einem höheren Automatisierungsgrad in einer schlankeren Struktur mit weniger (Personal-)Ressourcen. Der zweite Archetyp wird stark von den Mitarbeitern im Management Accounting getrieben und initiiert (Bottom-up). Hier geht es darum, die Nutzung der Daten durch innovative Analysemethoden zu verbessern, zusätzliche Datenquellen zu integrieren und von neuen Technologien wie der künstlichen Intelligenz zu profitieren. Von den fünf untersuchten Unternehmen konzentrieren sich drei auf Bottom-up-Veränderungen, ein Unternehmen wendet einen Top-down-Ansatz zur Effizienzsteigerung im Management Accounting an, und das letzte Unternehmen konzentriert sich nicht auf eines von beiden, sondern weist Merkmale beider Archetypen auf.

Die Ergebnisse zeigen, dass die Digitalisierung des Management Accountings weitgehend mit der Gesamtstrategie des Unternehmens übereinstimmt. Einerseits wird das Management Accounting in einer Phase der Kostenreduktion wie jede andere Funktion behandelt, in der Prozesse automatisiert und Kosten nach Möglichkeit reduziert werden. Zum anderen wird es in einer Wachstumsphase des Unternehmens als eine vorteilhafte Unterstützung strategischer und operativer Entscheidungen behandelt.

Contents

Abbreviations

BI	Business Intelligence
CEO	Chief Executive Officer
CFO	Chief Financial Officer
e.g.	For example
ERP	Enterprise Resource Planning
EUR	Euro
HR	Human Resources
ICT	Information and Communication Technology
IT	Information Technology
KPIs	Key Performance Indicator
p.	Page
pp.	Pages
R&D	Research & Development
RPA	Robotic Process Automation
RQ	Research Question
SSC	Shared Service Center

List of Figures

Introduction

1

Digitization has been heavily discussed both in society and the business context (World Economic Forum, 2016). In society, the focus has been placed largely on the impact on the overall job market. Within companies, management accounting researchers and practitioners investigate the impact of automation and the introduction of new tools that can benefit management accounting. The discussion breaks down into various jobs and functions within a firm. Digitization of management accounting is gaining importance in practice because new technologies change the way management accountants work and enable them to conduct their tasks differently.

Technologies like big data enable management accountants to analyze large amounts of data when supporting decision-makers. Also, processes are being further automated with the help of, for instance, robotic process automation (RPA). Furthermore, the digitization of management accounting triggers needs for changes in organizational setups and in the skills and backgrounds of management accountants.

This study analyses the impact of digitization on the management accounting function. Previous studies touch upon this subject without conducting in-depth empirical research. Hence, from that starting point of conceptual discussion, this study applies a qualitative case-study approach to gain further understanding on the subject based on the gathered empirical data.

As Al Htaybat and von Alberti-Alhtaybat (2017) state, most studies in the field of management accounting and digitization appear to be rather conceptual. Their work is one of the first comprehensive empirical studies to be published in a major research journal within the field of management accounting. The focus of the study is solely on big data and corporate reporting, excluding other tasks of management accounting, such as planning and decision support. Peters et al. (2016) and Kelton and Pennington (2012) provide some of the first empirical evidence regarding

O. Holtkemper, *Digitization of the Management Accounting Function*, Controlling und Rechnungslegung – Managerial and Financial Accounting, https://doi.org/10.1007/978-3-658-31509-2_1

selected aspects of management accounting digitization. Focusing on the effects of business intelligence (BI) quality on performance measurement and the effects of information presentation format on investor decision-making, their studies indicate that new (digital) innovations and developments can have an impact on management accounting. For instance, Peters et al. (2016) find in their empirical study that the quality of a BI system enhances the diagnostic and interactive dimensions of management control systems. Additionally, Trigo, Belfo, and Estébanez (2014, p. 1) argue that "Real-time accounting needs new technological answers" and propose the further use of solutions like cloud computing and business intelligence. However, no in-depth empirical work examines the status quo in practice and the potential effects of these new solutions. Therefore, there is still significant empirical work to be done in this specific field of research.

Quattrone (2016) bases his argument in favor of the future need for management accounting in companies on the statement that digitization does not provide solutions for perfect information and completely rational decision-making. Hence, he expects management accounting to gain importance again in the organizational context (Quattrone, 2016). In addition, Janvrin and Watson (2017) argue in their conceptual study that even with big data, the aim of accounting will not change, which is to derive and provide information to internal and external decision-makers.

Against this background, this study analyzes how the management accounting function has been and is expected to be impacted by digitization by understanding how companies have been reacting to this technological shift.

1.1 Motivation

Concerns about the impact of digitization on industries, company functions, and organizational units are raised from various stakeholders like associations, employees, and politicians. Comments and opinions range from a positive stance (digitization as an opportunity) to a risk for certain industries, companies, corporate functions, and jobs. As is the case for other disciplines, management accounting experts and researchers discuss the potential impact of digitization on this function. Management accounting and management control associations publish articles and organize events for discussions around digitization in an attempt to shed light on the topic and to suggest solutions for the future.

Discussions on business practices also hint at the importance of the topic. Management accounting in most companies is a major source of both financial and non-financial data that is relevant for analyses and decision-making. Management accounting professionals are typically also aware of previous analytical works and analyses that can be incorporated into the decision-making process. The practical importance of management accounting for decision-making is, hence, also reflected in the importance of the discussion around its digitization. In the process of data exchange and discussions, there are significant differences between companies in how they use modern technologies and tools in management accounting. Hence, it is important for companies to get to know and learn from what other companies are implementing in terms of management accounting digitization. Also, digitization is a widespread phenomenon, occurring across different industries, meaning industries could learn from each other. From the practical viewpoint of management accountants, there is a high level of curiosity (even fear) with regard to how management accounting is affected by digitization. Furthermore, managers from various functions that depend on the decision support from management accountants are interested in understanding how digital technologies can support their functions and how it might change decision support processes and provide opportunities to improve daily decision-making. Additionally, related conferences indicate that in research and in practice, management accounting digitization is being discussed intensely and is expected to have a significant impact.

Thus, this need for research on the topic from a practical and scientific point of view led the author to take on this research project to contribute to academia and to scientific fields, as well as the practitioners' community.

1.2 Objective, Research Questions, and Framework

As mentioned, the motivation for this research project was derived from a practitioners' view, as well as from the academic research gap. The goal is to analyze the impact of digitization on management accounting using a qualitative approach to further develop the knowledge of the topic and to provide practitioners with insights on how other companies' management accounting functions are affected by and deal with digitization.

1.2.1 Research Questions

The key research questions were derived based on the literature review presented in Section 2 and on discussions with management accounting professionals. The overarching question of professionals and academics is: How is management accounting impacted by digitization? Based on this general question, four research questions were derived.

The first research question deals with the tasks of management accounting in a digitized function and the tools that the management accountant applies to fulfill tasks. In other words, the question deals with the impact of digitization on *what* is done in management accounting. A potential shift of focus in current tasks as well as possible new tasks of management accountants are discussed. Tools already introduced and technologies expected to have an impact on management accounting are part of this research question. Literature discusses the impact of digitization on management accounting tasks and tools only to little extend. For instance, Quattrone (2016) discusses how decision-making processes change on the one hand, but on the other hand also argues that even new tools might not provide perfect information. Another study, Janvrin and Watson (2017), also argues that the goal of (management) accounting remains the same, providing information to decision makers. Overall, existing studies touch upon the point and discuss the importance without analyzing cases in a detailed way. Hence, the first research question is:

RQ1: How are tasks and tools of management accounting functions impacted by digitization?

The second research question deals with the impact of digitization on *where* the tasks are conducted. The question refers to (expected) organizational changes due to digitization as well as to potential corresponding geographical changes. Recent studies hint at some changes in how management accounting might be organized within companies. For instance, Marchant (2013) argues that management accountants might develop in their organizational setup towards being members of the core strategic team. Overall the studies indicate that there might be a change in the organizational setup of management accounting due to digitization. However, only little empirical evidence is provided. There is a research gap on how the organizational setup of management accounting is affected by digitization. Hence, the second research question is:

RQ2a: How is the organizational and geographical setup of management accounting impacted by digitization?

The second part of RQ2 concentrates on the drivers and barriers of digitization in management accounting. Here, the question deals with factors that have or could have an impact on how digitization affects management accounting. Existing studies do not focus specifically on drivers and barriers of digitization in management accounting. There is a gap in empirical research on the drivers and barriers. Hence RQ2b follows:

RQ2b: What are the major drivers and barriers when it comes to the implementation of digitization in the management accounting function?

With the third research question, this study seeks to determine the skills management accountants need to possess to succeed in times of digitization. In addition to how skill requirements and profiles change, the question focuses on how the skills can be obtained by management accountants and graduates. The emphasis is on how companies can recruit and train their management accountants. Previous studies suggest, that different skill sets might be needed in the future for management accounting to master their job and that accounting classes and teaching resources might need to be adjusted (Gamage, 2016; Sledgianowski et al., 2017). However, little research conducted includes different perspectives on how skills, backgrounds and trainings might change. Hence, this study involves the perspectives of practitioners and enablers, such as Human Resources, in order to answer the third research question:

RQ3: How are the required educational backgrounds and skills in management accounting impacted by digitization?

For the overall question on the impact of digitization on management accounting, the relation to a firm's strategy is investigated. The author seeks to find how the strategic direction and change in strategy impact the digitization of the management accounting function in the manufacturing companies at hand. Literature indicates a link between strategy and management accounting practices of a firm (Gerdin & Greve, 2004; Guilding, 1999; Lachmann et al., 2013; Langfield-Smith, 1997). However, there is little research on how the impact of digitization on management accounting is related to the strategy of the firm. Hence, based on that gap in research the fourth research question has been derived:

RQ4: How is management accounting impacted by digitization and how does the impact relate to the overall strategy of the firm?

1.2.2 Research Framework and Process

Key digital trends were identified based on publications and conferences of practitioners, as well as experience within the field. As detailed in the methodology section, the focus of this study encompasses several topics that are relevant to each other rather than a single subject. From the preliminary interviews and readings, it appears that management accounting researchers and practitioners are not sure which technology or trend will have the most impact on management accounting. Additionally, the interdependencies of trends and technologies were important aspects during the research process (Ax & Greve, 2016; Brandas, Megan, & Didraga, 2015; Janvrin & Watson, 2017).

Leaving out one part or focusing on a single aspect in isolation would lead to over-simplifying the analysis. For example, an analysis of big data without considering how the data is collected and which technologies can be used to analyze data would not be feasible and would reduce the explanatory power of the analysis. Furthermore, the discussion in this study was built on three pillars: tasks and tools, organizational changes, and backgrounds and skills required. This was determined based on the learnings from preliminary interviews, which revealed that the roles and responsibilities are not (yet) as affected by big data or digitization as the three pillars mentioned.

1.2.3 Research Process and Evolvement of Research Framework

In the course of the interview process, the framework was detailed and adjusted based on findings where necessary. As described in the methodology section, case study research can be applied as an iterative process in which the author keeps reviewing and adjusting the approach and questions based on findings from the data already collected. The same applies to the theoretical underpinning of the study and its findings. During the data collection and analysis, the author moved between theory and data (in an explorative manner) to make sense of the findings.

One of the aspects that stood out early on in the interview process was the transformational processes in the motivations behind digital change. This procedural perspective is relevant for all the research questions.

The detailing of the research framework was only possible during the course of the interviews because the steps of the process (i.e., standardization/consolidation, transfer to shared service centers, automation, and implementation of new analytical tools and systems) and especially the comparability of those steps between the cases were first discovered during the initial interviews. As mentioned in the literature review, other studies do not take this procedural perspective into consideration. This is where the explorative approach stands in strong contrast to quantitative research in which theories and hypotheses are fixed before data collection.

1.3 Structure of This Dissertation

The dissertation is divided into six sections, starting with this short introduction. The author then reviews the existing literature and critically discusses former studies on the impact of digitization on management accounting to derive the four research questions. Based on the findings of the review, the research gap is revealed. The theory section then explains the theoretical concepts used to design and conduct this study. Theoretical considerations on driving digital change are described from two perspectives: the individual employee in management accounting and the firm/organization as a whole. These theoretical concepts were analyzed before and during the empirical work to explain the empirical findings from the interviews. The methodology section explains the methodology applied and provides the reasoning for choosing a qualitative and explorative research approach for this study. Here, the author uses the concept of grounded theory and critically reviews and applies the criteria of case study measurement. This section also provides details on the research design and process, the setup of the interviews, and the companies used for this multiple case study. Finally, the author describes the empirical findings with regard to the research questions. Based on the findings from the five case studies, two archetypes of management accounting digitization are derived. Additionally, a futuristic view on management accounting is developed based on the interviews conducted with management accounting software providers. After describing the empirical findings, the author critically discusses them along with the contributions of this study against the background of the existing research.

1.4 Contribution

This study contributes to existing research in several ways. First, it provides a framework to analyze the impact of digitization on management accounting, which is highly relevant for practitioners as well as researchers (Al-Htaybat & von Alberti-Alhtaybat, 2017; Bhimani & Bromwich, 2009; Quattrone, 2016). In contrast to other studies, a comprehensive framework of four questions has been derived to answer the overarching question on the impact of digitization on management accounting.

Based on the framework, the author critically reviews existing studies and sets them into context. Furthermore, the author relates academic research on the topic to practitioners' work in such places as companies, conferences, and fairs. This approach contributes to the field of research because practitioners and researchers have reported a gap between company practice and current topics in management accounting studies.

Based on previous studies, the empirical work provides detailed evidence by conducting in-depth case studies in different companies. It is the first major study to provide empirical evidence on the impact of digitization on management accounting based on five case studies. By doing so, the author contributes to the research in the field, as well as to information that management accountants can refer to when discussing and shaping their future role in their organizations.

The triangulation of perspectives within the cases by interviewing not just management accountants or experts but also enablers (i.e., information technology [IT] and human resources [HR]) and internal customers (e.g., sales managers and production managers) ensures that all relevant views are covered. Hence, biases and subjectivity can be reduced. This methodological feature differentiates the study clearly from the majority of other studies, such as Sledgianowski, Gomaa, and Tan (2017), Ax and Greve (2016), and Beaman and Richardson (2007), which focuses on the view of management accountants or other experts/academics related to the field.

Based on the framework and the empirical work, archetypes of digitization in management accounting were derived. Additional empirical work in the future can build upon the framework and, for instance, could further test the archetypes in a quantitative setting.

Additionally, this study can be helpful on a broad basis, as findings are not limited to one country or industrial sector because all the case companies have international operations and are based in various manufacturing industries, such as pharmaceuticals & chemicals, mechanical engineering, consumer goods, and automotive suppliers. Thus, in contrast to previous studies, which partly focus on one industry or geographical background, these findings contribute to research on a broad set of industries and countries.

Overall, this study provides input for further research to be conducted in this field. Further research could consider expanding this methodology into a longitudinal study by conducting interviews of the same nature in the future and comparing the status of today with those findings. By doing so, researchers could also evaluate if the expectations mentioned in this study regarding the future of the management accounting function hold true.

Literature Review and Research Gap 2

In this section, after describing the review methodology, the relevant literature is analyzed, and the research questions are thereby derived.

To establish a common understanding of the research questions at hand, major terms and definitions are provided in the first part of this section because "management accounting" and especially terms like "digitization" are often used in a broad context.

One of the aims of this study was to conduct research that is relevant for science and company practice not only to explain the phenomena of digitization but also to address the challenges and opportunities it brings for management accounting. More practically, it endeavors to provide insights to management accountants who are dealing with the impact of digitization or are responsible for the reshaping of the management accounting function in an organization. Thus, the author has also reviewed papers and publications that have not been published in a scientific context but rather in practice-oriented outlets later in this section. The decision to review these publications was taken during early preliminary discussions with management accountants, as it became obvious that there is a significant discrepancy between the published scientific research and the changes happening in the practice of management accounting.

2.1 Definitions and Clarifications

Digitization is a widespread expression frequently used by researchers and practitioners. Hence, this section breaks down the term "digitization" into the relevant aspects for this study and defines the function of management accounting.

O. Holtkemper, *Digitization of the Management Accounting Function*, Controlling und Rechnungslegung – Managerial and Financial Accounting, https://doi.org/10.1007/978-3-658-31509-2_2

2.1.1 Management Accounting

"Management accounting" is a term used by many practitioners and researchers but not always precisely with the same understanding in mind. To establish a common base, a short definition and a differentiation from related items are provided in this subsection.

One definition of management accounting is an "analysis and provision of any financial and non-financial information to managers" (Burns et al., 2013). However, as definitions provided by management accounting institutions indicate, the term can be further specified when focusing on the job that management accountants conduct in practice. For instance, the Chartered Institute of Management Accountants (CIMA, 2005) defines management accounting as the "process of identification, measurement, accumulation, analysis, preparation, interpretation and communication of information used by management to plan, evaluate, and control within an entity and to assure appropriate use of and accountability for its resources. Management accounting also comprises the preparation of financial reports for non-management groups such as shareholders, creditors, regulatory agencies, and tax authorities" (Mancini et al., 2016, p. 14). This definition provides a detailed view of management accounting and shows that the role covers a broad set of tasks. The focus on the various tasks can be interpreted differently by companies, divisions, and management accountants. The priorities of management accounting depend on various factors like the size and structure of a company but also the expectations from managers within the company.

Additionally, it depends on the organizational objectives to what extent management accounting is involved in certain tasks. That is why management accounting can also be defined as that part of accounting that "produces information for managers within an organization. It is the process of identifying, measuring, accumulating, analyzing, preparing, interpreting, and communicating information that helps managers fulfill organizational objectives" (Horngren, Sundem, Stratton, Burgstahler & Schatzberg, 2008, p. 5). As indicated in the definitions, the target group of the information provided by management accounting is primarily the management team of a company. However, as hinted by the CIMA definition, the differentiation from financial accounting is not always distinct and depends on various factors such as the type of analysis at hand, structure of the company, and availability of expertise in different departments. In this study, the focus is on the provision of information to internal decision-makers such as managers and key account administrators.

The term "financial accounting" is strongly related to management accounting but should be differentiated. Financial accounting refers to accounting tasks related transactions with financial character. Tasks include recording and classification of transactions of an organization, but also the interpretation of the outcomes (Ahmed, 2008). The differentiation is important in this context because the impact of digitization on financial accounting could potentially vary from that on management accounting (and could be more disruptive). For instance, in management accounting, the analyzed data differ from financial accounting, the focus is on the future rather than the past, and the questions it deals with are diverse. Financial accounting, on the other hand, is strongly based on transactional financial data and, hence, is more strongly correlated to basic transactional accounting tasks (Horngren et al., 2013; Singh Wahla, 2011).

2.1.2 Digitization

Approaching the term from a technical perspective, digitization can be referred to as "the process of converting analog information into a digital format" (Katz & Koutroumpis, 2013, p. 314). In a corporate context, digitization refers to the capacity to "utilize digital technologies to generate, process, share, and transact information", (Katz & Koutroumpis, 2013, p. 314). Digitization builds on the advances in the technological fields, such as network access technologies, semiconductors and software engineering. It also leverages the opportunities resulting from the use of common platforms with the purpose of application development, e-commerce, and social networks (Katz & Koutroumpis, 2013). However, not all aspects of digitization are directly relevant to management accounting. Nevertheless, if the business model of a company is affected due to digitization, management accounting will also be affected indirectly, as one of its main functions is to support decision-making in the process of changing business models.

Digitization also increases the availability of data that impact management accounting because more relevant data is available for decision support. In addition, technological developments could have an impact on management accounting in the form of digitization. One of the obvious reasons is the increase in the use of information technology (IT) and information and communication technology (ICT). However, in the context of digitization of the management accounting function, technological developments such as artificial intelligence, big data, and RPA are also discussed. In this explorative study, the author left the definition of digitization as broad as described here, as it became obvious that the digitization of management accounting cannot be reduced to one single technology or trend.

2.1.3 Digitization: Further Discussion on Terms and Definition

Especially in German-speaking countries, terms and definitions with regard to digitization are discussed in detail. To avoid misinterpretations, the discussion here is focused on the differentiation between the terms digitization and digitalization. Based on the technical definition provided above it is obvious that digital transformation is based on digitization. Digitization can be defined as generating a digital record of analog and physical documents such as images, paper documents, and photographs. In this definition, the term refers to the process of converting something from a non-digital format into a digital format (Brennen & Kreiss, 2016; Feldman, 1997). Digitalization can also mean "turning interactions, communications, business functions and business models into digital ones" (Brennen & Kreiss, 2016, p. 557). Digitalization in business requires the digitization of information in order to, for instance, adjust processes into digital processes. In science and in practical discussions, the term "digitization" is used for both the definitions provided (digitalization and digitization). Hence, for the sake of consistency with other studies and sources used, the author uses the term "digitization" in this study.

2.1.4 Management Control

Another crucial definition that should be established before analyzing the impact of digitization on management accounting is that of management control. Merchant and van der Stede (2017, p. 7) state, "Management control involves addressing the general question: Are our employees likely to behave appropriately?" This question can be decomposed into the following: "Firstly, do employees understand what is expected of them? Secondly, will they work consistently hard and try to do what is expected of them (i.e., will they implement the organization's strategy as intended?)? Thirdly, are they capable of doing the job? Finally, what can be done to solve management control problems" (Merchant & van der Stede, 2017, p. 7). Based on these questions, one can tell that management control and management accounting are closely related. However, the objectives differ, as management accounting aims to support business decisions and the monitoring aspect of decisions, whereas management control aims to control and guide the management team. In this study, the focus is not on tasks and roles concerned with management control but on management accounting. Nonetheless, when conducting interviews and interpreting findings, one should have in mind that the management accountant might also conduct analyses with the aim of management control rather than decision-making in the sense of management accounting. When it comes to reporting tasks, for instance, the reports and data provided might have management accounting as well as management control aspects. Hence, this (potential) overlap needs to be taken into consideration when engaging with management accountants.

2.1.5 Controlling vs. Management Accounting

Because most of the case companies included in this study have their headquarters and origin in Germany, it proves helpful to clarify definitions and differences in "controlling" (as it is generally referred to in Germany) and "management accounting" (as it is referred to in the Anglo-Saxon context and literature).

Although the term "controlling" is borrowed from the English language, it does not solely refer to "management control" (in the Anglo-Saxon context), as its first impression portrays. Rather, the Anglo-Saxon counterpart to German controlling is "management accounting" (see Hoffjan, 2008; Sheridan, 1995; Willson, Bragg, & Roehl-Anderson, 2003). There is a high overlap in the tasks and roles.

However, there are some differences that should be kept in mind when conducting a study with conglomerates having their origin in Germany. The central difference between Anglo-Saxon management accounting and German controlling is the underlying database. Whereas in Germany, the use of the dual-circle system separates the data of external accounting from that of controlling, in the Anglo-American context, a uniform database is used for external and internal reporting purposes (Hoffjan, 2008). Anglo-Saxon management accounting also focuses on shareholders, whereas German controlling mainly addresses internal target groups. There are further significant differences. For instance, management accountants in Great Britain and the United States are involved to more detail in operational tasks. Also, the range of duties is broader (Hoffjan, 2008).

However, in addition to the already existing overlap, in recent decades, a strong convergence of international controlling and management accounting systems brought the two terms even closer together (Granlund & Lukka, 1998; Hoffjan, 2008; Shields, 1998). This is due to the increasing use of international reporting standards, globally integrated markets, and the worldwide application of IT (e.g., enterprise resource systems from Germany). In the broader context, management accounting and controlling aim at similar targets: providing information, participating in the management process, and ensuring rational decision-making (Hoffjan, 2008).

Because the interviews were conducted in German, the term "controlling" as in the German context was used instead of "management accounting." Tasks of controlling differ between companies, as they do for management accounting. In some companies in Germany, controlling is focused on financial aspects, with some companies conducting bookkeeping from within controlling departments. However, the focus in this study (as described earlier) is on management accounting tasks. Hence, this differentiation was introduced to interviewees to determine the impact of the digitization of financial controlling/accounting tasks.

2.2 Literature Review Methodology

To identify relevant articles, a comprehensive keyword search was carried out at the beginning of the research process in March 2017. First, relevant journals were searched. Second, search engines such as Google Scholar and those of university libraries were used to identify relevant literature. This search was conducted manually by the author. The keyword search was at first restricted to English publications and international journals.

According to Webster and Watson (2002, p. xiii), the major contributions to a field of research can be "assumed to be published and discussed in the leading journals of the corresponding field of research." Hence, the focus while reviewing literature was first on major management accounting journals, such as *Management Accounting Research*, *Journal of Accounting and Economics*, and *Journal of Management Control*.

Based on the articles identified in the first steps, the author reviewed the citations included in those articles. By doing so, previous research was considered along with studies that appeared in adjacent fields and scientific journals that may be of relevance to this study (Webster & Watson, 2002).

In addition to scientific journals, non-scientific articles were reviewed and considered to enhance the preparation for the interviews, as preliminary discussions with management accountants pointed out that scientific research lags behind the current progress in management accounting. Hence, the aim of this literature review was to set the existing literature into the context of the research questions, which are relevant for both scientists and practitioners.

2.3 Literature Review Results

2.3.1 Impact of Digitization on Management Accounting

When it comes to the impact of digitization on management accounting, overall, the literature tends to focus on conceptual findings. Scholars are aware that more empirical research needs to be done (Al-Htaybat & von Alberti-Alhtaybat, 2017; Arnaboldi, Busco, & Cuganesan, 2017; Jeacle & Carter, 2011; Scott & Orlikowski,

2012). Furthermore, the lack of a precise definition and scope of digitization in the context of management accounting was noticeable among existing literature. In this rather new field of research, few articles have been published in highly ranked journals to date. Understandably, because digitization is a result of technological advancement, its application and impact are relatively new phenomena to research. Nevertheless, a few articles were found to be relevant and revealed interesting findings, contrasting the publications and discussions of practitioners. Only a limited number of comprehensive papers exist, which also include the empirical analyses of the impact of digitization on management accounting.

For example, Al-Htaybat and von Alberti-Alhtaybat's (2017) work is one of the first comprehensive empirical studies to be published in a major research journal. Interviews with experts were conducted and reveal some opportunities and risks that big data provides for accounting and reporting, in particular. The focus of the authors was only on big data and reporting, rather than on other tasks and aspects of management accounting, such as planning and decision support. The authors conclude that big data enables corporations to apply a different approach to reporting with regard to the timing and accuracy of information. Additionally, the prospective element of reporting could be further improved using big data. As the authors state, there is still much empirical work to be done in this field of research. Additionally, from an objective point of view, one can conclude that the perspectives covered by the authors concentrate on management accounting, as all interviewees were experts and employees in the field of management accounting, with a focus on interviewees from the scientific field. No external or other related viewpoints were covered in the interviews. Al-Htaybat and von Alberti-Alhtaybat's (2017) study is also the first to provide a literature review on the impact of big data on (management) accounting.

Quattrone's (2016) is another major study approaching the question of how management accounting is being impacted by digitization. The study stresses the significance of management accounting for decision-making in a new era and argues that even with digitization, a perfect information setting cannot be achieved. Hence, according to Quattrone (2016), the importance of decision-making processes is expected to remain high and, therefore, management accounting will also maintain great importance. The author sets the impact of digitization on management accounting into historical and cultural contexts and points out that management historically is a profession focused on the derivation of knowledge for decision-making (Quattrone, 2016). Quattrone (2016, p. 1) argues that "while the effects of the digital revolution on management accounting and decision-making are still unclear, these effects surely (and hopefully) will not deliver the dream of perfect information and rational decision-making as one may be led to believe by the growth of data-driven organizations and societies." With his argument, Quattrone (2016) clearly points out his expectation and hope, showing that he could be biased in his opinion because he is defending management accounting as his discipline. However, his argument is not backed by empirical evidence. Even though the argument is future-oriented, an analysis of management accounting and other parties could have added to the value of this study and, hence, be used as motivation to confront practitioners with the research question of this study.

Bhimani and Bromwich (2009) provide another interesting view on the change of the decision support task of management accounting. The focus of the study is on changes in the decision-making process and corresponding transformations in the organizational structure. The authors anticipate that "organizational complexities do not allow clear distinction between decision making thinking and actions" (Bhimani & Bromwich, 2009, p. 41). Thus, a change in organizational structure is foreseen. They expect rather fluid structures of departments and teams. In this context, they point out that due to the new digital economy, strategy formulation and actions are strongly intertwined. They expect management accountants in the future to be part of management teams. Additionally, strategic management accounting and other approaches are discussed. The authors argue that new technologies will be used regardless of whether accountants are involved. Interestingly enough, the authors ask management accountants to more actively "address issues raised by modern day globalization and digitization forces" (Bhimani & Bromwich, 2009, p. 42).

For the purpose of this study, it is an interesting proposition with regard to the (expected) change. The study authors ask how management accountants expect the change to go and what role they play in the change. Bhimani and Bromwich (2009) request management accountants to play a more proactive role in the firm and in the way the management accounting function is developed, rather than waiting for an external impact that might have negative consequences.

Another relevant study is that of Moorthy et al. (2012, p. 1), who analyze the "use of Information Technology (IT) in management accounting and potentials and drawbacks of adopting IT in management accounting." Because IT can be seen as an important enabler of digitization, the study is highly relevant. Several potential benefits and drawbacks in adopting IT in management accounting are mentioned. For instance, the increase in the speed of information provision (up to real-time data) and the ability of the accountant to focus on important tasks are described as potential benefits. In addition, the authors argue that the introduction of IT into management accounting provides a competitive advantage. Major drawbacks could be the high investment and maintenance costs of the new systems, as well as the requirement for highly skilled workers (Moorthy et al., 2012).

One claim of the study is that there is a "need for a shift in accountants' education by increasing the knowledge of information systems and IT knowledge" (Moorthy et al., 2012, p. 1). This argument is especially relevant for the research question regarding the impact on educational background, required skills, and training. Overall, the authors recommend that management accounting change more frequently. They criticize that "IT changes frequently and accounting standards remain for many years without any major change" (Moorthy et al., 2012, p. 1) and underline the potential that IT and digitization have for management accounting. In their opinion, IT may help "improve accounting department efficiency and produce results effortlessly, timely and accurately" (Moorthy et al., 2012, p. 2). Figure 2.1 shows key literature reviewed by the author. However, additionally further studies related to the field have been reviewed, which can be found in the bibliography section.

2.3.2 Impact on Tasks and Tools (RQ1)

The first research question deals with the impact of digitization on the tasks and role of management accounting. This research question was derived based on the analysis of the existing literature and the gaps identified. Published research provides limited evidence on how the tasks and tools of management accountants are (expected to be) impacted by digitization. Recent studies focus on limited aspects. For instance, Janvrin and Watson (2017, p. 1) argue that the main goal of accounting remains the same, to "create and provide information to internal and external decision makers." Although the authors refer to accounting in general and not specifically to management accounting, the argument is relevant for management accounting, especially with regard to internal decision-makers. Janvrin and Watson (2017, p. 3) refer indirectly to tasks and tools by arguing that new resources (e.g., "free datasets, software tools and cases") should be included in the classrooms of accountants, which reversely means that accountants are expected to apply new tools to their job. Hence, this study suggests that there might be an impact from digitization (at least from big data, which is the focus of their study) on accounting overall, which implies that it is the case for management accounting, as well.

As mentioned earlier, Quattrone (2016) assumes the continued importance of management accounting in decision-making due to the absence of perfect information, even with new (digital) tools and processes. The argument of the author shows that change is likely with regard to tools—in other words, digitization is expected to have an impact on management accounting tools. However, he points out that the task of management accounting in providing and analyzing information will persist because decisions could still be made directly without preparation by management accounting.

These arguments are used as a starting point for a discussion that leads to the question of what the impact on tools and tasks looks like in practice.

Bhimani and Willcocks (2014) describe opportunities with and potential difficulties caused by big data in relation to management accounting information provision. The authors point out that "traditionally presumed sequential and linear links among corporate strategy, firm structure, and information systems design are no longer in play" (Bhimani and Willcocks, 2014, p. 1). One can conclude from the argument that big data will also have an impact on the work of management accountants because it is directly related to these three factors.

Another interesting argument is provided by Marchant (2013), who discusses the future role of management accountants. In Marchant's (2013, p. 3) view, management accountants will more and more be "core members of the strategic team, using their skills and capabilities in information management and analytics". By pointing out that only those with the best analytical capabilities will stay relevant, Marchant (2013) underlines the strong focus on analytical tasks which he expects for management accountants in the future.

Talha, Raja, and Seetharaman (2010) argue in a similar direction. They highlight the unfolding of proactive management accounting combined with a tendency of management accountants to become part of the management team. In other words, they also expect management accounting tasks to be more closely related to management decisions. Their request for highly proactive management accounting also strengthens the argument that management accounting needs to demonstrate its value in a company and to progress in the way it conducts its work to avoid becoming redundant.

With regard to studies referring to the research question concerning the tools of management accounting, several relevant articles were identified. However, a low depth of analysis on how the specific tools and technologies will change the work of management accountants can be concluded.

For instance, Brandas et al. (2015) provide a technology comparison with respect to accounting information systems (AISs). The authors look into the potential of cloud and mobile technologies, which provide the opportunity to share and collect information in a new way (Brandas et al., 2015) for accounting information systems. Because management accountants can be expected to work with AISs, this development will also impact their work.

Trigo et al. (2014) describe technologies that enable the application of real-time accounting (e.g., cloud computing and BI). Real-time accounting is described as an answer to managers' needs for more up-to-date information in fierce competition. Depending on the industry a company is competing in and the questions management accounting is dealing with, real-time accounting could prove helpful, especially for industries like (fast-moving) consumer goods. Hence, for the case companies interviewed for this study, real-time accounting could be relevant.

Another important technological development is self-reporting tools, such as dashboards. When developing a dashboard, four phases of introduction can be distinguished. First, the relevant indicators for the dashboard are selected. Second, the data sources are identified. Third, the ability to drill down into the indicators with the dashboard to identify cause-and-effect relations is introduced. Lastly, functionality for forecasting and scenario analyses can be enabled (Lachmann & Wenger, 2012). In the context of this study, the progress of the introduction of tools like dashboards is discussed to understand the status quo in practice and the new developments and features that have been recently introduced.

Finally, a recent study by Peral et al. (2017) describes how data mining techniques can be applied to identify relevant key performance indicators (KPIs). This technological opportunity has an impact on the tools and tasks of management accounting because it allows for the improvement of the KPIs used in a company based on data. Overall, the studies reviewed provide valuable input for the interviews and touch upon crucial topics. Suggestions for technologies and trends (e.g., real-time accounting, mobile, and virtual currencies) that could be relevant for management accounting are provided, although empirically not investigated. In sum, one can say that published research provides limited evidence on how the tasks and tools of management accountants are (expected to be) impacted by digitization. Still, the importance and relevance of the impact of digitization in different contexts on the tasks and tools of management consulting are discussed. However, the narrow focus of those studies demonstrates the relevance of the first research question: **How are tasks and tools of management accounting functions impacted by digitization?**

2.3.3 Impact on Organizational Setup (RQ2)

With regard to the impact of digitization on the organizational setup of management accounting, limited research has been conducted and the topic is only partly addressed. One reason might be that to answer the question of the organizational setup, the question on the change in the relevant tasks of management accounting needs to be answered first. Another possible explanation could be that the impact of digitization on the management accounting organization is simply not as relevant as one might suggest.

Phillips and Halliday (2008) analyze synergies between marketing and accounting. By doing so, they touch only slightly on the digitization of management accounting. They present empirical evidence of "de facto leadership being taken by the IT function to the detriment of what might otherwise have been developed: a synergistic relationship between the marketing/accounting planning interface and business performance" (Phillips & Halliday, 2008, p. 3). In the future, this de facto leadership could mean that the IT function will have an even greater impact on other functions like management accounting because of their dependency on the expertise and support of the IT function. This is one reason why, in the interviews conducted for this study, the perspective of support functions such as IT was considered.

Beaman and Richardson (2007) investigate the potential tendency of accounting functions to be limited to "financial reporting and transaction processing, rather than decision support and problem-solving", (Beaman and Richardson, 2007, p. 59). Their empirical study shows that management accountants spend two thirds of their time resources on financial reporting and transaction processing. While researching the tasks of and skills needed in management accounting, the authors hint that if this function does not focus further on management accounting activities, this might have organizational consequences. For instance, other functions with the required skill sets in IT and data analytics might take over tasks and roles within organizations that could reduce the value of their management accounting teams.

As described earlier, Marchant (2013, p. 1) argues that "management accountants will increasingly find themselves as core members of the strategic team using their skills and capabilities in information management and analytics to develop and maintain the distinctive capabilities of their organizations". Indirectly, the argument indicates that there might also be organizational changes. For instance, the management accounting team could be integrated further into operational units to be organizationally closer to the management team it supports. However, Marchant (2013) did not go into further detail on this topic.

Overall, the number of studies related to this question and their depth indicate that the prior empirical evidence is limited. For the interviews of this study, this was taken into consideration because the discussions on RQ2 might, therefore, have a different direction than, for instance, those on RQ1 due to the variation in the depth of previous research. In sum, one can conclude from the literature that digitization might change the organizational setup of management accounting. However, limited empirical evidence is provided by existing studies on what those organizational changes might be (if they happen). Hence, there is a research gap with regard to how experts and practitioners expect the organizational setup of management accounting to develop. Based on that, the second research question of this study follows: **How is the organizational and geographical setup of management accounting impacted by digitization?**

Another factor that has not been discussed in recent literature is what drives or impedes change with respect to the digitization of management accounting. Existing studies do not detail drivers and barriers of digitization in management accounting. Hence, the second (closely related) part of the second research question focuses on drivers and barriers of change: **What are the major drivers and barriers when it comes to the implementation of digitization in the management accounting function?**

2.3.4 Impact on Educational Background, Required Skills, and Training (RQ3)

The question on how the requirements regarding the educational background, required skills, and training of management accountants is covered to a fair extent (compared to the other research questions) in recent literature.

In the identified research, studies were conducted on what type of skills need to be acquired and how universities should adjust their curricula. However, the question on how organizations can prepare and educate their existing workforce for the digital era is not touched upon in detail. Out of the research questions, this one addresses the background of management accountants and their required skills to the highest degree. The need for an adjustment of the accounting curriculum and the improvement of IT skills of employees in (management) accounting is emphasized. However, the majority of the articles refer to accounting in general, not specifically to management accounting.

For instance, Gamage (2016) suggests that big data should be included in accounting classes to provide accounting graduates with big data capabilities. The study also shows how accounting bodies and academia try to implement the big data related content in their courses. Sledgianowski et al. (2017) use the Competency Integration for Accounting Education framework to describe content and material on technologies which could be taught in accounting classes. Examples of big data and information systems integration into instructional resources are provided (Sledgianowski et al., 2017).

Kaye and Nicholson (1992) analyze the use of computer in accounting over time and relate the findings back to an educational framework. The use of educational support tools is analyzed against the background of different ways of implementing these tools into classes. Spraakman et al. (2015) analyze the requirements regarding technology competencies when hiring management accounting graduates. The authors conducted an exploratory field study based on interviews with chief financial officers (CFOs) and their direct reports in New Zeeland. The results of their interviews indicate that graduates possess only intermediate proficiency with some Microsoft tools but enough familiarity with enterprise resource planning (ERP) systems.

Beaman and Richardson (2007) determine IT skills needed for decision support systems and explore how to display these skills in accounting education. Also, Moorthy et al. (2012, p. 1) claim that there is a "need for a shift in accountants' education by increasing the knowledge of information systems and IT knowledge." According to Moorthy et al. (2012), management accountants should acquire skills in such areas as computer usage, data modeling, forecasting and projections, developing assumptions and criteria, creativity, adaptability, and strategy formulation. Obviously, many of these skills were crucial in times before digitization but the list provides a first impression on what new skills could be required (e.g., stronger data modeling skills and a technology orientation).

Overall, the studies at hand suggest the skills that (management) accountants could need to master their job in the future, which forms the basis for the discussion of skills with the interviewees in this study. Any empirical work in the previous studies focuses on the perspective of management accountants and experts in the field. Therefore, to fill the gap of perspective, in this study, the viewpoints of other functions such as HR are also covered (see Section 4.5). As described previously, existing studies tend to focus on how educational institutions (e.g., universities) can prepare graduates better for the job of management accountant. There is only limited literature on how companies can develop their (existing) teams to be able to cope with challenges in digitization. Hence, the skills and background needed in management accounting are discussed in detail using perspectives from practitioners and enablers such as HR within a company to answer the third research question: **How are the required educational backgrounds and skills in management accounting impacted by digitization?**

#	Authors	Year	Title	Content/ key findings/ quotes	Journal
1	Diane J. Janvrin, Marcia Weidenmier Watson	2017	"Big Data": A new twist to accounting	- Authors argue that the main goal of accounting (even with Big Data) is still the same: create and provide information to internal and external decision makers - Authors identify resources to incorporate Big Data into the classroom (links to free datasets, software tools, cases, and class slides)	Journal of Accounting Education
2	Deb Sledgianowski, Mohamed Goma, Christine Tan	2017	Toward integration of Big Data, technology and information systems competencies into the accounting curriculum	- Paper uses the lens of the Competency Integration for Accounting Education framework to provide examples of Big Data and information systems integration into instructional resources. - Authors frame instructional resources using accounting course subjects as the unit of analysis.	Journal of Accounting Education
3	Michela Arnaboldi, Cristiano Busco, Suresh Cuganesan,	2017	Accounting, accountability, social media and big data: Revolution or hype?	- Paper outlines an agenda for researching the relationship between technology enabled networks – such as social media and big data - and the accounting function. - Paper surveys the existing literature and proposes ways in which to frame early and future research. - Findings: Three areas of investigation are identified: new performance indicators based on social media and big data; governance of social media and big data information resources; and, finally, social media and big data's alteration of information and decision-making processes.	Accounting, Auditing & Accountability Journal

Fig. 2.1 Key readings reviewed

#	Authors	Year	Title	Content/ key findings/ quotes	Journal
4	Khaldoon Al-Htay-bat, Larissa von Alberti-Alhtaybat	2017	Big Data and Corporate Reporting: Impacts and Paradoxes	- Study investigates the phenomenon of big data and corporate reporting - Seeks to determine the impact of big data and the current big data state of mind with regard to corporate reporting, what accountant and non-accountant participants' perceptions are of the phenomenon, what the accountants' role is and will be in this regards, and what opportunities and risks are associated with big data and corporate reporting. - Three topics, or categories, emerged from the data analysis: the big data state of mind and corporate reporting, accountants' role and future related to big data, and perceived opportunities and risks of big data. - Features of a new approach to corporate reporting were identified and discussed. Furthermore, four paradoxes emerged to express inherent opposing positions of big data and corporate reporting, namely empowerment vs. enslavement, fulfilling vs creating needs, reliability vs. timeliness and simplicity vs. complexity	Accounting, Auditing & Accountability Journal
5	Paolo Quattrone	2016	Management accounting goes digital: Will the move make it wiser	- Digitization of management accounting in general - Importance of management acc. for decision making in new era - Argues that even with Digitization no perfect information achieved and rational decision making will be impossible - Hence the improtance of decision making processes is still high (and therefore mgmt. acc. is still of importance)	Management Accounting Research

Fig. 2.1 (continued)

#	Authors	Year	Title	Content/ key findings/ quotes	Journal
6	Gary Pan, Poh-Sun Seow	2016	Preparing accounting graduates for digital revoloution: A critical review of information technology competencies and skills development	- Critical review of information Technology competencies and skills development based on literature review -Argument: Surge in demand for advanced IT skills among accounting professionals	The Journal of Education for Business
7	Christian Ax, Jan Greve	2016	Adoption of management accounting innovations: Organizational culture compatibility and perceived outcomes	- Examines the adoption of mgmt. acc. innovations at firm level - Authors develop and test an adoption model which draws on two recently introduced ideas about innovation adoption—the notion of compatibility between organizational culture and the values and beliefs embedded in innovations, and the perspective that early and late adopters might both be motivated to adopt based on expected economic and social gains and losses. - Authors assume that a diffusing innovation that is compatible with a firm's values and beliefs is adopted early if it is perceived as delivering adequate gains while the innovation is rejected if it is not perceived as doing so, and that a diffusing innovation that is incompatible with a firm's values and beliefs is adopted late if it is perceived as reducing the likelihood of incurring losses while the innovation is rejected if it is perceived as not doing so. - Hypotheses are generated and tested using data provided by a web-based survey of Swedish manufacturing firms on the diffusion of the balanced scorecard across those firms. - In most respects, the pattern of results this study finds supports the model and assumptions	Management Accounting Research

Fig. 2.1 (continued)

#	Authors	Year	Title	Content/ key findings/ quotes	Journal
8	Pandula Gamage	2016	Big Data: are accounting educators ready?	- Explores latest developments in Big Data and impact on accounting education. - Reviews Big Data developments with specific reference to the accounting profession. - Presents Some of the initiatives taken by the professional accounting bodies and universities to address Big Data topics in the accounting curriculum - Proposes that Big Data topics be embedded in existing courses across accounting curricula to prepare twenty-first-century accounting professionals with skills related to Big Data analytics	Accounting & Management Information Systems
9	Tony O'Brien	2015	'Accounting' for data quality in enterprise systems	- Organisations are facing ever more diverse challenges in managing their enterprise systems as emerging technologies bring both added complexities as well as opportunities to the way they conduct their business - study proposes an integrated framework that organisations can adopt as part of their financial and management control processes to provide a mechanism for quantifying data problems, costing potential solutions and monitoring the on-going costs and benefits, to assist them in improving and then sustaining the quality of their data.	'Accounting' for data quality in enterprise systems
10	Claudiu Brandas, Ovidiu Megan, Otniel Didrag	2015	Global perspectives on accounting information systems: mobile and cloud approach	- Article on Mobile and cloud accounting information systems (AIS) - Quantitative research on exisitng literature - Authors synthesize the potential of cloud and mobile technologies in the AIS and provide a SWOT analysis of the technologies in the context of AIS	Procedia Economics and Finance

Fig. 2.1 (continued)

#	Authors	Year	Title	Content/ key findings/ quotes	Journal
11	António Trigo, Fernando Belfo, Raquel Pérez Estébanez	2014	Accounting Information Systems: The Challenge of the Real-Time Reporting	- Study on real-time reporting - Selection of technologies presented which can help implemenation of Real-time accounting (e.g. business process mgmt., mobile devices, cloud computing, BI) - Real-time accounting and reporting addresses Need of managment for more updated information in order to be able to compete	Procedia Technology
12	Bhimani, Alnoor ; Willcocks, Leslie	2014	Digitisation, 'Big Data' and the transformation of accounting information	- Article discusses a model for understanding data, information and knowledge relationships. - Authors apply the model to examine developments in strategy, organisational and cost structures, digitisation, business analytics, outsourcing, offshoring and cloud computing. - Organisations need to be sensitised to different types of knowledge, the challenges in creating and applying that knowledge, and be more circumspect about what can be achieved through advances in information-based technologies and software - Big Data' and data analysis techniques enable executives to act on structured and unstructured information but such action must recognise that the traditionally presumed sequential and linear links among corporate strategy, firm structure and information systems design are no longer in play.	Accounting and Business Research
13	Güney, Aysel	2014	Role of Technology in Accounting and E-accounting	- Necessity of inclusion of information era and technologic factors in education for accountants described - E-Accounting introduced as one exemplary digital application	Accounting and Business Research

Fig. 2.1 (continued)

#	Authors	Year	Title	Content/ key findings/ quotes	Journal
14	Andreea Gabriela PONORÎCĂ, Ahmed H. Juhi AL-SAEDI, Hamza H. SADIK	2014	The impact of enterprise resource planning systems on management accounting	- Impact of ERP systems on financial reporting and management accounting analyzed - Results: ERP systems are not so well connected with the field of financial reporting analysis, but strongly linked with the management accounting field	Procedia Technology
15	Moorthy, M. Krishna; Ong Oi Voon; Samsuri, Cik Azni Suhaily Binti; Gopalan, M.; King-Tak Yew	2012	Application of Information Technology in Management Accounting Decision Making	- This study analyzes the use of Information Technology (IT) in management accounting and also the potentials and drawbacks of adopting IT in management accounting - Need for a shift in accountants' education by increasing the knowledge of information systems and IT knowledge	International Journal of Academic Research in Business & Social
16	Alnoor Bhimani and Michael Bromwich	2009	Management accounting in a Digital and Global economy: the Interface of strategy, technology and cost information	- Org. complexities do not allow clear distinction between thinking and actions in decision making - Change in organizational structures (e.g. "fluid" structures between departments/teams but also between organizations) - Digital and global economy compress together strategy formulation and actions - mgmt. accountants in the future possibly rather part of mgmt. teams - Strategic mgmt. accounting and other approaches discussed - techniques will be used (if accountants are involved or not) - Argument that like organisations, the management accounting field itself must address issues raised by modern day globalization and digitization forces	Oxford University Press

Fig. 2.1 (continued)

#	Authors	Year	Title	Content/ key findings/ quotes	Journal
17	Tsai, Chih-Fong	2007	On Classifying Digital Accounting Documents	- Study on digital accounting documents - Examines flat non-hierarchical and hierarchical classification schemes for automatic classification of different types of digital accounting documents (e.g., invoices, purchase orders, checks) - The experimental results show that non-hierarchical classification of digital accounting documents performs better than hierarchically classifying digital accounting documents	International Journal of Digital Accounting Research

Fig. 2.1 (continued)

2.3.5 Relation of Strategy and Management Accounting (RQ4)

Research question 4 focuses on how the digitization of the management accounting function is related to the overall strategy of the firm, which can be generally defined as a "plan for interacting with the competitive environment to achieve organizational goals" (Daft, 2016, p. 59). Management accounting can be described as a means to implement the strategy of the firm (Chenhall & Langfield-Smith, 1998; Lachmann, Knauer, & Trapp, 2013; Nyamori, Perera, & Lawrence, 2001). The digitization of management accounting could thus affect how this function supports the implementation of the firm's strategy.

Literature suggests that there is a connection between the types of strategy and management accounting practices of a company. In that context strategy is described as contextual variable of management accounting (systems) (Gerdin & Greve, 2004; Guilding, 1999; Lachmann et al., 2013; Langfield-Smith, 1997). Hence, one could assume that there is also a link between the digitization of management accounting (which potentially changes management accounting practices, processes, and tools) and the strategy of the firm (Chenhall, 2003; Lachmann et al., 2013; Quattrone & Hopper, 2005).

Thus, based on the theories and studies described, changes in management accounting (i.e., also the digitization of management accounting) might relate to changes in the overall strategy (and vice versa). However, in the literature reviewed, little research was conducted on how the impact of digitization on management accounting is related to the strategy of the firm. To fill this gap in the literature, the fourth research question was derived and discussed in the interviews: **How is management accounting impacted by digitization and how does the impact relate to the overall strategy of the firm?**

2.4 Review of Practitioners' Papers and Publications

Publications by practitioners discussing the impact of digitization on management accounting are also reviewed for this study. The viewpoints of practitioners are highly relevant because the authors are working in management accounting and, hence, can report changes in their daily work. Practitioners tend to analyze and discuss relevant topics in a more forward-looking manner compared to the majority of the scientific articles, which focus on the past or present (this is also due to the nature of the scientific approach). Technological introductions like big data and Industry 4.0 are the focus of practitioners' papers and publications. The topic has also been widely and controversially discussed in conferences over the last few years.

In addition to curiosity about what might come in the future, there is a fear of management accounting becoming less important or even obsolete in its current form (Wiegmann, Tretbar, & Strauß, 2014). Use cases often indicate that management accounting has a supportive role or acts as a moderator for the introduction of new technologies and analytic capabilities. Authors require that management accountants ask themselves about their future role instead of waiting for other functions to introduce big data solutions, management accounting should aim for being the expert in the company for applying big data analytics (Weichel & Herrmann, 2016).

Because many companies introduce new departments or teams to address digital topics, management accountants must safeguard their role as decision support and data experts rather than merely processors of financial transactions or bookkeepers. If management accounting does not adjust accordingly, its relevance will inevitably decrease. Transactional and bookkeeping-related tasks will be further automated (for instance, via RPA), as well as reporting. Weichel & Herrmann (2016, p. 9) describe how management accountants could benefit from big data, which is "large volumes of (unstructured) data as well the technologies that are applied for data processing and analysis of data." Weichel & Herrmann (2016) mention some (mainly positive with regard to management accounting) changes that are expected, including that big data will help improve reporting and analyses and refine planning and forecasting. Furthermore, the decision-making process in companies is expected to quicken with the increasing availability in data and analyses.

In addition, the author states a variety of challenges that management accountants face in an effort to benefit from big data, including limited internal capacity for data processing. Weichel & Herrmann (2016, p. 10) see a "need for quick access and processing/analysis of data". Finally, Weichel & Herrmann (2016) point toward the lack of expertise in data management, which is apparent in many management accounting departments.

Other studies focus on different aspects of digitization and their impact on management accounting. For instance, Grothe (2016) points toward opportunities that come with the new amount of data gathered in management accounting and related functions. Specifically, Grothe (2016) underlines the ability to recognize risks and issues related to the potential default of a business partner earlier than in the past due to patterns that can be recognized in the data.

Wiegmann et al. (2014) provide insights on the effect of IT trends on the role of the management accountant and conclude that they provide more opportunities than risks for this function. For instance, they describe the benefit of releasing management accountants from repetitive tasks. IT trends (e.g., the use of mobile technology and new visualizations) also enable management accountants to generate more interest from management regarding their analyses. Self-services allow managers and other users of information to conduct their own analyses. However, a risk for management accountants is that the value-add of their work could become less visible (Wiegmann et al., 2014). Value-add could be any extra information or knowledge gained by a stakeholder due to the service provided by management accounting.

On the other hand, other studies argue that with the increasing use of self-reporting, management accounting still has the important task of debiasing decision-making processes (Weber & Schaeffer, 2016). Weber and Schaeffer (2016) discuss several debiasing techniques, including the formalization of decision-making processes, which is often applied in practice. Management accounting takes the role of ensuring that decision-making processes are formalized even when self-service reporting is introduced. Formal decision-making processes aim at rationalizing decisions and detain managers from making biased decisions based on their preferences.

Overall, the reviewed papers and publications by practitioners reveal interesting findings. However, one must keep in mind that the approach applied for those publications is not always scientific and arguments could be biased due to the role these authors have in their company. For instance, a management accountant writing an article that is published could be biased because he does not want to offend his peers. For the purpose of this study, the insights and information obtained were taken into consideration for the derivation of the interview guidelines and the research framework. However, for the reasons previously mentioned, only a selection of articles was referred to in this section.

2.5 Confirmation of Research Gap

As previously mentioned, existing literature focuses on conceptual findings rather than empirical research. Additionally, prior studies do not precisely define or provide the scope of digitization in the context of management accounting.

One can conclude that for this rather new field of research, few studies have been published in highly ranked journals. There is only a limited number of comprehensive papers that also include an empirical analysis on how digitization impacts the management accounting function.

The latest studies published in the area explicitly mention a further need for research in the field of management accounting digitization (Al-Htaybat & von Alberti-Alhtaybat, 2017). With regard to the research questions, it is evident that the required skills (RQ3) have been discussed and analyzed to a higher degree than the content of the first two questions (RQ1 and RQ2). Although the question on how tools and tasks are impacted by digitization is discussed, empirical evidence has largely not been taken into consideration. The studies and arguments shared in journals point rather toward the discussion of management accounting's future relevance than on the impact of digitization. Organizational changes are only researched to a limited degree, as well.

Overall, the limited number of papers, the lack of depth in empirical analyses, and the propositions of the authors themselves indicate that there is a research gap regarding the impact of digitization on management accounting, especially with regard to empirical research in the context of companies.

3 Theory

When conducting qualitative research and compiling case studies, theoretical considerations before collecting data and theoretical explanations of the empirical findings play an important role. In this study, the research on theory was intended to help prepare the interview guidelines. In addition, the emerging patterns and findings have been related back to theories. A theoretical framework was established to help choose the right methodological approach for this study.

This section discusses theories that have been applied in the economic and management accounting context and can be used to explain potential motivations and reasoning behind changes conducted in the context of digitization. In this explorative study, the author switched between the empirical data and potentially relevant theories to make the most sense of the findings.

Because the research on this topic is still in an early stage, there is no established or specific theory that explains the impact of digitization on management accounting. Hence, existing theories are applied to explain the findings and discuss the approach. Ultimately, the intention of this study is to derive a theory or concept based on the data. In the context of the developments in management accounting through digitization, the motivation and objectives of different stakeholders play an important role. For instance, the motivation of a management accountant to provide information on the latest trends and topics is expected to be higher than that of an employee from the IT function who is supporting management accounting in the process of digitization. When preparing the interviews and conducting preliminary talks with experts in the field, one major aspect emerged: perspectives from individuals (potentially from different functions in a company) can differ from those of the organization as a whole. The organizational perspective focuses on the potential

O. Holtkemper, *Digitization of the Management Accounting Function*, Controlling und Rechnungslegung – Managerial and Financial Accounting, https://doi.org/10.1007/978-3-658-31509-2_3

reasoning and motivation regarding the company as a whole when considering digitization and respective measures. It thus provides a theoretical basis for discussing company strategy in the context of this study. The individual perspective points toward theories explaining the motivation behind the behavior of individuals within a group and on the decision-making of individuals in general.

3.1 Organizational Perspective

Changes in a firm, such as the digitization of management accounting, can be viewed from an organizational perspective as well as the perspective of the individual (i.e., employee) who might be triggering or affected by the change. The organizational perspective focuses on the collective point of view. Based on the principal-agent theory, one can argue that from this perspective, the principal has a predominant role in driving changes that benefit the company as a whole (Eisenhardt, 1989; Jensen & Meckling, 1976; Prendergast, 1999). Digitization in this context is driven by the motivation to benefit the company as an organization. Initiatives that might be opposed by individual employees in management accounting (e.g., further automation of processes or cost-reduction initiatives) will be supported by the principal because cost-savings maximize the company's economic benefit. The argument to optimize the efficiency of the management accounting function is also supported by theories and concepts related to the division of labor (Smith, 1778) that encourage the separation of tasks and delegation of processes to workers who have specialized skills to complete those tasks more efficiently. The aim of the division of labor, in the context of digitization, is to achieve economies of scale and scope that can be better leveraged in shared service centers. Local management accounting units, however, are too small to specialize at a sufficient level to achieve these economies (Silvestre, 1987).

3.1.1 Division of Labor and Economies of Scale and Scope

In the theory of the firm, the division of labor has been applied to argue in favor of firms focusing on and specializing in specific value chain steps and for the specialization of individual employees within a function or process. By doing so, the company can increase its output with the available resources. In this context, economies of scale refer to the cost advantages that arise with the increased output of a product. The theory, also often associated with the term experience curve, argues that production costs fall with the accumulated production volume. The inverse relationship between quantity produced and per-unit fixed costs, allows companies to benefit from economies of scale (Henderson, 1968).

In the context of this study, the concept is applied not to manufacturing processes but to management accounting processes. Within a management accounting team, standardized processes can be divided and split among team members in a way that allows the members to focus on specific tasks, such as a certain type of report or the support of a specific business function. The organizational perspective is especially relevant for RQ1 and RQ2 on the impact of digitization on tasks and tools and the organizational setup of management accounting. For example, the support regarding creating reporting dashboards can be centralized. The shared service center employee will be able to specialize and produce more output at the same fixed costs. Additionally, this employee will create economies of scope because he will cover multiple tasks, whereas a local employee would only create one dashboard of relevance for the local management.

3.1.2 Porter's Generic Strategies

The theory on competitive strategies is detailed in the context of this study as part of the organizational perspective to gain a better understanding of how measures of digitization relate to the overall strategy of the firm. According to Porter (1985, p. 1), two factors underlie the choice of a competitive strategy, which "aims to establish a profitable and sustainable position against the forces that determine industry competition". The first deals with the attractiveness of an industry for long-term profitability and its associated factors. Porter's (1985, p. 2) structural analysis of industries and the "five competitive forces that determine industry profitability" can be used to obtain this information. The second factor according to Porter (1985) addresses how the relative competitive position of a company within an industry is determined.

The focus in the theoretical framework of this study with regard to competitive strategy is on the second factor and the competitive strategies that Porter (1985, 1998) defines to explain competitive positioning within an industry (Joannidès de Lautour, 2018). The reason for this is that the case companies researched in this study are established players and have been in their industries for decades and, as Porter (1985) argues, firms do not have much influence over their industry attractiveness. The choice of competitive strategy, however, has the potential to "improve or erode a firm's position within an industry" (Porter, 1985, p. 2). Two basic types of competitive advantage that, combined with the scope of activities used to gain them, lead to three generic strategies for achieving above-average performance in an industry: cost leadership, differentiation, and focus (see Fig. 3.1). The focus strategy has two variants: cost focus and differentiation focus. Cost leadership and differentiation strategies aim to achieve a competitive advantage in several segments, whereas focus strategies seek an advantage in one narrow segment (Porter, 1985).

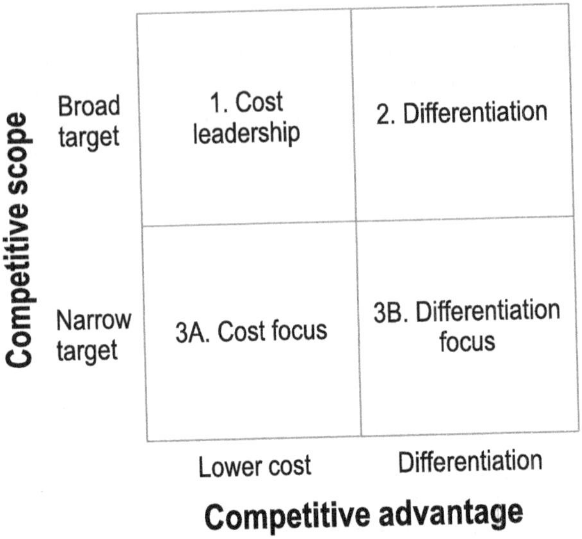

Fig. 3.1 Generic strategies (Porter, 1985)

In the cost leadership strategy, companies aim at becoming the producer with the lowest costs in the industry. As mentioned, the companies operate within a broad scope, targeting many industry segments. Some companies with a cost leadership strategy may operate in different but related industries. Sources of cost advantage vary according to the structure of the industries but the key to success for a low-cost producer is to identify and benefit from all the available sources (Joannidès de Lautour, 2018; McGahan & Porter, 2002; Montgomery & Porter, 1991; Porter, 1985). In the context of management accounting digitization, one source of cost advantage is the ability of a firm to benefit from automation and, hence, a reduction of the human workforce in management accounting, for instance.

In a differentiation strategy, a company aims to be unique in its industry along dimensions that are deemed important by customers and positions itself to fulfill those needs. Because the attributes are valued by buyers, their fulfillment may be rewarded with a higher willingness to purchase. The ways to achieve differentiation vary by industry (Porter, 1985). In the context of this study, a differentiation strategy could be supported by digitization in management accounting through which a company could benefit from a data analysis and distinguish itself in offering more suitable solutions to its customers based on that analysis.

The third strategy, which is the focus strategy, has two alternatives. In the cost focus, a company aims for a cost advantage in its target segment. In contrast to that a firm with a differentiation focus aims at a differentiation position. Both alternatives rely on differences between the specific target segments and other segments in the industry. Porter (1985, p. 15) states that the "target segments must either have buyers with unusual needs or else the production and delivery system that best serves the target segment must differ from that of other industry segments." Furthermore, the cost focus is based on differences in cost behavior in some segments, whereas the differentiation focus exploits the special needs of buyers in certain segments (Porter, 1985). In this study, again, the theory is applied to analyze how this strategy relates to the digitization of management accounting.

Porter's generic strategies framework is applied to relate the measures of digitization in management accounting to the overall strategy of the firm. This will indicate whether the impact of digitization changes with the different overall strategies of firms and, if so, how the impact differs. Hence, this theory framework on strategy is relevant for both the overarching question on how digitization impacts management accounting and how the impact of digitization relates to the strategy of the firm (RQ4). As indicated in the literature review, there is some research on the impact of management accounting on strategy and vice versa. This research project aims to add to this topic by further exploring the impact of digitation on that relationship.

3.2 Individual Perspective

On the individual level, theories and concepts have already been developed and applied prior to digitization gaining the prominence it has today in business literature, some of which can be used to describe potential patterns that the process of the digitization of the management accounting function could trigger.

A crucial assumption of many management control research studies is that organizational members are self-interested agents who prioritize their own objectives over those of the organization (Eisenhardt, 1989; Jensen & Meckling, 1976). Therefore, based on this theory, the digitization of management accounting (e.g., automation of processes and implementation of new tools and technologies) is assumed to be affected by the motivation and self-interests of the employees involved in the process. In a case in which an employee expects negative consequences for himself from a change initiative, the employee would not be likely to support or even hinder such an initiative when involved in the process. In contrast, any changes deemed beneficial by the individual would be supported. For instance, a sales representative who wishes to receive regular and timely reports would support the automation of the reporting process, as that is deemed beneficial to himself. However, a project manager who spends a majority of his working hours producing reports manually could oppose the same initiative, as it could make his work redundant.

The argument based on the principal-agent theory is supported by the expectancy theory. The expectancy theory argues that people in a firm are willing to invest more effort when they think that this will lead to a good performance and hence to a reward they value (Vroom, 1964). Thus, an employee in management accounting will drive aspects of digitization that are expected to benefit his performance. By introducing new tools that allow for a better analysis of data or by integrating new sources of data, the employee might aim to improve the analyses submitted to the management team.

The social exchange theory, which proposes that relationships people value and focus on are those which they expect the highest rewards from while minimize our costs can also be classified into the individual perspective (Blau, 1964). This theory can be applied to explain priorities and differences in prioritization from various perspectives when discussing the digitization of management accounting (see Section 3.2.1 on social exchange theory).

Another stream of literature considered in the context of the individual perspective is on the decision-making theory, which emerged from the field of behavioral economics and psychology. Studies on human bias in judgment and decision-making assume that human brains tend to fall for certain fallacies and cognitive biases, which lead to irrational decision-making (Kahneman & Tversky, 1979). One of many examples is the confirmation bias, which describes the tendency for people to seek out or interpret information so that it confirms their beliefs. With respect to decision-making in times of digitization, machines support the interpretation of information without the fallacies of the human brain. However, because software is mostly programmed by humans, one must consider that there might also be biases grounded in the coding behind the software, as discussed in management accounting literature regarding automation tools in decision processes, which might cause new biases (e.g., recency bias).

In this context, Weber and Schaeffer (2016) propose debiasing techniques (e.g., the introduction of formal decision processes). If certain repetitive decisions are made based on objective criteria, decision support through software might decrease the biases in decision-making processes because once the machine learns the assumptions and criteria, it will not be influenced by other factors that could impact human decision-making. For example, the pricing negotiation process that a sales representative leads could be supported by software that calculates a price range based on a previously determined algorithm (considering variables such as volume, manufacturing costs, and customer volume history). The support of the tool provides the sales representative with a price range that is free from other soft factors, such as the general mood and atmosphere of the discussion, which could influence the sales professional to offer higher or lower prices outside the optimal price range.

In contrast to the organizational perspective, the individual perspective helps explain the view of digitization from the perspective of a specific employee in the management accounting function. Theories described in this section are applied to discuss potential intentions of management accountants when implementing or driving digitization in their function and also when describing their point of view and expectations obtained during the interviews.

3.2.1 Social Exchange Theory

Social exchange theory is often applied when analyzing the behavior of human beings who are co-working or exchanging thoughts or goods. Social exchange happens whenever an individual interacts with others. Hence, it applies when individuals from the management accounting function interact within the function to install digital technologies in their work as well as with other functions that are involved in the change process and in the daily work (e.g., users of the information that management accountants provide and supporting functions such as IT and HR, which ideally support management accounting in preparing for and incorporating digital change). However, one must note that social exchange exceeds the basic economic model of costs and rewards. It suggests that humans feel positively or negatively about relationships through a combination of three methods: cost-benefit analyses, comparison level, and comparison level of alternatives. For these three methods, both extrinsic and intrinsic factors play a role. The basic idea is that relationships that provide the most benefits for the least amount of effort are the ones we value the most and are likely to keep in the long term (Blau, 1964; Homans, 1958).

According to this theory, humans are self-centered and not necessarily concerned with equality. In this specific context, the theory can be applied from different points of view. All actors involved in the complex relationship aim to maximize their own benefit. For instance, the management accountant could be expected to trigger the aspects of digitization that benefit him the most or try to inhibit change that is expected to have a negative impact on his job, career, or tasks.

The same logic can be applied to internal customers of the management accountant, such as a key account manager. The internal customer will only favor change and investments in new tools that he expects to directly and positively impact his work. Their support might also depend on the past experiences and relationships that the internal customers have had with the management accountant. If the internal customer has the perception that the output from the analyses and reports provided by management accountants is helpful in decision-making, he might help trigger the change.

Other important parties involved are the supporting functions, who (as single individuals) are also expected to maximize their own benefits. An employee in the IT function (when supporting the introduction of a new tool), for instance, might favor a tool that requires the least additional effort or complexity for his support tasks rather than introducing a new tool that is provided by a new supplier on a different platform that is more complicated but is likely to be a better solution and to improve the management accountants' work output.

In this context, the direction of change can also be an interesting factor to consider because the change could be driven by the management accounting function and employees themselves. However, in other organizations, a holistic program driven by corporate management and IT could be also applied to the management accounting function. For those companies in which the implementation of new tools is driven by the management accounting team, social exchange aspects influence such factors as the implementation grade and speed of implementation of the new tools. Management accountants might only implement what is beneficial for their role.

However, when imposed by other functions, the situation and impact might differ. For example, the automation of tasks could be driven in a more drastic way when initiated from outside the function compared to when driven by management accountants, who might be more protective when it comes to automation and the corresponding headcount reduction.

3.2.2 Decision-Making: Heuristics and Biases in Decision-Making and Human Judgment

One of management accounting's major tasks is to support management in decision-making by providing information, analyses, and recommendations. The research of Tversky and Kahneman (1974) on heuristics and biases of the human mind regarding judgment under uncertainty provides a helpful understanding of the psychology of decision-making. They found that heuristics are used to reduce mental effort in decision-making, but they can lead to systematic biases or errors in judgment. Heuristics are not necessarily negative for decision-making but can help reduce the effort and time in making a decision. However, under certain conditions, heuristics can include biases that can lead to making the wrong or less-optimal decision.

Tversky and Kahneman (1974) describe three major heuristics in their work on judgment under uncertainty: representativeness, availability, and anchoring and adjustment. Representativeness refers to the finding from their experiments that "[w]hen no specific evidence is given, prior probabilities are utilized properly; when worthless evidence is given, prior probabilities are ignored" (Tversky & Kahneman, 1974, p. 1125). The availability heuristic describes a situation in which "a person evaluates the frequency or the probability of events by availability, i.e., by the case with which relevant instances come to mind. The reliance on the availability heuristic leads to systematic biases" (Tversky & Kahneman, 1972, p. 207). The anchoring and adjustment heuristics describe situations in which "people make estimates by starting from an initial value that is adjusted to yield the final answer" (Tversky & Kahneman, 1974, p. 1128). What makes this approach problematic is that "the starting point … may be suggested by the formulation of the problem, or it may be the result of a partial computation. In either case, adjustments are typically insufficient" and, hence, the approach does not lead to the correct solution to a task (Tversky & Kahneman, 1974, p. 1128).

This theory stream is helpful for the discussion of the impact of digital technology on the decision-making process, including its potential to improve the process in the business context by reducing the risk of falling for these biases. It applies in this research context because decision-making in a company often occurs under uncertainty—decisions are made without all the necessary information available.

For some specific questions, problems, and tasks, machines will soon be able (if they are not already) to not just provide advice but to make decisions themselves. In this study, this argument is analyzed with respect to the automation of processes and the application of artificial intelligence. A higher level of automation in decision preparation and decision-making might lead to a reduction of biases because, for instance, when deciding on a price for a certain customer, a manager might have previously based it on a gut feeling but with the help of historic pricing data, cost data, and further information, the manager can obtain a clear price recommendation from an analytical tool.

However, digitization can also create new biases. For instance, as discussed earlier, when introducing self-reporting, managers could be biased in their decision-making process. For example, recency effects could cause managers to prioritize more recent information in their decision (Tversky & Kahneman, 1973). Hence, research suggests that the increasing use of self-reporting requires management accountants to remove bias from decision-making processes (Weber & Schaeffer, 2016).

Artificial intelligence applied in (management) accounting might go one step further and include and combine information in the decision-making process that the human mind cannot process or produce. Hence, in referring to the representativeness and availability heuristics, technology could help overcome these issues because machines do not follow the patterns of the human mind.

Overall, this decision stream is applied to back up the questions around decision support, which could be improved by machines, helping overcome the heuristics and biases described by Tversky and Kahneman (1974). In this research context, the theory is relevant for RQ1 regarding the tasks of management accounting, especially the decision support task. However, it is also relevant for the other tasks of the management accountants because whenever a human being makes decisions, heuristics and biases can play a role, which can affect tasks such as manually compiling a report and preparing budget figures.

3.3 Conclusions from Theory

The theory section elaborated on major theoretical themes from concepts that have been applied to the context of digitization on management accounting. There is no single theory that can be applied to and cover the topic. If there was, a quantitative approach could have been adopted to test the established theories, constructs, and previous findings. However, based on the theory research, a qualitative approach is preferential. Overall, a theoretical framework consisting of several theories is necessary due to the complexity of the overarching research topic, the fact that no single theories applies to the field, and the inclusion of four different research questions in this study. The arguments and concepts analyzed within the individual and organizational perspectives indicate the issues and topics that should be expected when interviewing parties involved at the case companies.

The arguments in the organizational and individual perspectives were taken into consideration when organizing, conducting, and analyzing the interviews. The organizational perspective, which incorporates concepts from psychology (e.g., heuristics in decision-making) and strategy, helped in the preparation of the interviews and in reaching conclusions from the empirical findings. Because strategy is expected to have an impact on management accounting and vice versa, it was necessary to first analyze the economic situation of each company along with their implemented strategic directions. For instance, when a company openly communicated cost-cutting measures or directly described itself as a cost-leader in a market, it gave a good indication as to how digitization is being implemented and its impact on management accounting. The argument that different parties and individuals involved aim to maximize their own benefit and the discussion on how decision-making in times of digitization can change with respect to reducing the fallacy of human biases were taken into consideration when organizing the interviews (e.g., by covering different perspectives within the same company).

Methodology

4

4.1 Qualitative vs. Quantitative Research

As analyzed in the literature review section, few studies in the field of management accounting digitization have been conducted and published. For a quantitative approach to be taken, previous work to base hypotheses on would be necessary. Because this is not the case, a qualitative approach was chosen to pave the way for further research in the field. The qualitative research approach provides "data about real life people and situations" (de Vaus, 2014, p. 6) and is, hence, helpful for shedding light on the developments in management accounting caused by digitization. The author chose a case study approach to explore and compare how manufacturing companies approach the challenge of digitization in their management accounting function.

Qualitative research seeks to contextualize and gain a better understanding to answer the research questions. A qualitative method is appropriate for this research since it helps to establish a better understanding of background and experience of the interviewees and their view of how digitization impacts the way they work as management accountants or how they work with management accountants (in the case of the internal client and support functions such as IT and HR). This research project allows participants to describe the changes they have already experienced and are expecting in the future. The study derives detailed accounts of the participants' experiences. Furthermore, existing studies have not provided validated constructs that could have been used in a quantitative study in this context. Hence,

Electronic Supplementary Material The online version of this chapter (https://doi.org/10.1007/978-3-658-31509-2_4) contains supplementary material, which is available to authorized users.

O. Holtkemper, *Digitization of the Management Accounting Function*, Controlling und Rechnungslegung – Managerial and Financial Accounting, https://doi.org/10.1007/978-3-658-31509-2_4

deriving a construct based on qualitative research allows future researchers to apply a quantitative approach.

4.2 Research Design: Methodological Framework

The methodological framework of this study is based on the grounded theory concept (Glaser & Strauss, 1967). Grounded theory describes both a method of scientific work and a set of tools that can be used to develop a data-based (i.e., interview-based) theory (Strauss & Corbin, 1998).

One major assumption for choosing the grounded theory methodology is that not all concepts that deal with the phenomenon of interest have been discovered and identified, at least not in this population and this place (Strauss & Corbin, 1998). The questions of this study meet these criteria and characteristics, thus making the grounded theory methodology an appropriate choice. Grounded theory offers a set of useful guidelines and suggestions for analysis techniques. However, it does not provide strict instructions to follow.

At the beginning of the research process is an unbiased stance regarding the approach. This does not mean that all prior knowledge and background information must be ignored but that the fieldwork is conducted without any solid concept or theory in mind. Potentially relevant concepts and theories will be taken into consideration at a later stage during the process of research and analysis, when the findings are also compared to existing theories.

The data selection process is not linear but recursive; in other words, the findings at every step of the project are reflected upon and applied to those discovered at the project's beginning. The analysis of the data and further case collection will be done at a point in the future when saturation is reached. A triangulation of data and methods was applied to shed light on the research topic from different angles. Data triangulation, in this case, refers to the inclusion of alternate data sources, such as different times, organizations, and persons.

4.2.1 Application of Grounded Theory and Case Study Methodology

As mentioned, this multiple case study is developed based on the concept of grounded theory. The research process followed was based on the work of Strauss and Corbin (1998) and Eisenhardt (1989), who describe in detail how to build theory from case studies.

The majority of the data stems from the interviews conducted. Additionally, data from observations (e.g., during the demonstration of a tool), informal conversations, and documents provided by the case companies were included in the database. One important method of obtaining data was through notetaking during and after each round of interviews, which served to document key issues that stood out to the interviewer. In addition, the interviews were recorded with the approval of the interviewees—using a voice recorder that was placed openly on the table—and then transcribed. The data collection occurred from September 2017 to August 2018. Additionally, preliminary interviews via telephone served to introduce the researcher and the topic and to make a first assessment of the company's progress and approach regarding the digitization of management accounting.

During the collection of the data (i.e., the conducting of the interviews), the first steps of the analysis were completed. This led to certain decisions regarding how to proceed with the interviews. For the transcriptions of the interviews, information that was not necessary was excluded, such as casual conservation on irrelevant topics at the beginning or end of the interviews.

After the interviews, several rounds of coding were conducted. The process of analyzing the data also involved three levels or types of coding: open, axial, and selective (Strauss & Corbin, 1998; Tillmann & Goddard, 2008). Additional documents reviewed include annual reports, management presentations, and information provided by the companies on their homepages and investor relations portals. Because the author conducted the interviews at the companies' premises, he was also able to collect and review more data provided by the interviewees. For instance, at one company, a management accountant introduced the author to the planning and budgeting tool. Also, PowerPoint presentations and PDF files used internally at the companies to introduce new processes or to document change projects were shared with the author. Hence, by applying this approach of conducting interviews in person, the author was able to derive a vast amount of information related to the companies' management accounting that is not publicly available. These documents also have a positive impact on the objectivity of the data gathered because they are widely shared within the company and not just the opinion of single individuals.

4.2.2 Case Study Research Design and Process

A detailed case study research design was developed based on the methodology literature. According to Yin (2009), for case study research design, five elements need to be taken into consideration: a study's questions, its propositions, its units of analysis, the logic linking the data to the propositions, and the criteria for interpreting the findings. This multiple case study was defined and specified based on these five components.

With regard to the study's questions, case studies are most suitable for tackling how and why questions (Yin, 2009). As indicated in the introduction, this explorative study focuses on how questions that aim to find how the management accounting function has changed due to digitization in the case companies at hand. Hence, the first component to be taken into consideration is met. Another crucial component is the availability of study propositions, which allow to look for relevant evidence and move in the right direction (Yin, 2009). In this case study, the author developed and detailed the propositions in the literature research with the help of preliminary expert interviews before conducting the actual fieldwork.

The next major component is the unit of analysis, which Yin (2009, p. 30) states is "related to the way you have defined your initial research questions." In this case study, the unit of analysis are organizations; more specifically, small groups within these organizations—the manufacturing accounting functions. Additionally, there must be logic that links the data to the propositions by which good research design "can create a more solid foundation for the later analysis" (Yin, 2009, p. 34). Analytic techniques representing ways of linking data to propositions include "pattern matching, explanation building, time-series analysis, logic models, and cross-case synthesis" (Yin, 2009, p. 34). During the course of the data analysis as well as the preparation and setup of the interviews, the need for a logic link was taken into consideration and developed by switching between data and theory for sensemaking and by going back to interviewees when specific aspects needed clarification.

Additionally, the research design should provide for criteria for interpreting the findings (Yin, 2009), which the research process that was outlined at the beginning of the study supplied. The analysis and interpretation of the findings were conducted based on the research questions defined and the theoretical framework derived. Furthermore, the author needed to decide whether to conduct a multiple or single case study. Based on the preliminary interviews and the differences discovered between companies, the author decided to apply a multiple case design because the additional cases offered important insights for answering the research question that a single case could not provide.

4.2.3 Validity Tests

To ensure the validity of the case study for the phenomenon at hand, validity tests suggested by methodological experts were conducted (Yin, 2009). Construct validity, which evaluates whether the designated measurement method actually measures what it claims to, such as a question, hypothesis, or theory, has been tested using several sources of evidence for each case company. Interviewees were (with some exceptions due to timing issues) interviewed separately to ensure they provided independent opinions. Additionally, the results of the analysis were discussed with the interviewees at a later point in time to ensure that their statements were understood correctly.

Another important validity test is for external validity, which refers to the generalizability of the results (Yin, 2009). For multiple case studies, it is crucial to use replication logic. To ensure comparability, similar case companies were selected, and the same methodology was applied and documented rigorously. Finally, reliability tests were applied to ensure that the study methods, such as data collection processes, can be replicated by other researchers to obtain the same findings (Yin, 2009). To ensure reliability, interviews were conducted in the same manner for each case company. The resulting data was compiled in a database that included the transcripts, pictures taken (only when allowed by the case company), and documents provided or downloaded.

4.3 Case Selection

The selected case companies were chosen based on four sampling criteria: the universe, size, strategy, and sourcing (Robinson, 2014). The sample universe defined for this case study was limited to manufacturing companies to ensure the comparability of the business models. If companies from sectors such as financial services or transportation had been included, the comparability would have been lower. This also refers to the basic structure and tasks of the management accounting function of the companies. Manufacturing companies have within the management accounting function teams or experts to support the leaders of the production function, which is a unique characteristic that companies from non-manufacturing sectors do not possess. Also, the systems and tools used in the management accounting of a manufacturing company might differ. Other sets and sources of data are available, such as machine data, which could be used. Additionally, recent trends and changes in manufacturing (e.g., the Industrial and Internet of Things and Industry 4.0) could have an impact on the management accounting function. This aspect further differentiates manufacturing companies from other types of companies and could supply further interesting insights unavailable from non-manufacturing firms. Hence, for the context of digitalization, the differentiation between manufacturing and non-manufacturing firms could have an impact.

Furthermore, the cases were restricted to companies with at least EUR 1 billion in revenues to ensure a minimum and comparable company size. The assumption behind this criterion is that the structure and the work of management accounting in smaller companies differ to a significant extent from that of larger corporations. Another criterion for the selection of the companies was the internationality of their operations, that is, manufacturing, sales, and management accounting tasks are conducted by teams that are based in more than one country.

4.3.1 Determined Sample Size

When determining the sample size of the study, two major aspects must be balanced. On the one hand, the size must allow the researcher to actually conduct the research in practice given a certain time frame and further circumstances of the phenomenon, especially in digitization, in which changes are happening rapidly, and new findings are constantly being published (Robinson, 2014). Hence, the time period set to collect the data should not extend beyond a few months. On the other hand, the sample size must be large enough to enable the researcher to derive findings which allow to generalize (Robinson, 2014). Therefore, for this qualitative study with interviews to be conducted onsite, the sample size was thought through at the beginning of the research process and a minimum number of 3–4 detailed cases was determined based on the preliminary phone interviews. However, the upper limit was then identified during the research process when out of the cases conducted, patterns emerged and further preparational interviews with other companies did not provide major additional findings.

4.3.2 Sampling Strategy

The sampling strategy followed was in a purposive manner. Participants were selectively identified. When selecting individuals to participate, they should extend the knowledge of the researched phenomenon (Robinson, 2014). Specifically, participants were contacted based on the defined sample universe; the ability to extend the author's knowledge was judged based on preliminary interviews conducted with the management accounting representative of each case company (between 40–60 min each).

4.3.3 Sample Sourcing

Sample sourcing describes the process of sourcing and selecting the interviewees (Robinson, 2014). Management accountants were reached out to by the researcher based on their interest in the topic and their position in a potential case company. With those management accountants who were responsive, preliminary interviews were conducted via telephone to introduce the project and gather information on the digitization of management accounting in their companies.

In total, 28 interviews were conducted. Based on the preliminary interviews, five case companies were selected. As mentioned, these preliminary interviews were initial discussions conducted with one representative of the management accounting function to find out on a high level the current changes and projects in terms of the function's digitization in that company. Additionally, the purpose and context of this study were explained in those discussions to provide the companies with a basis for their decision to participate. For each company, an interview day at its headquarters was scheduled to personally conduct the interviews in familiar surroundings. For each case company, the digitization in management accounting was analyzed from three perspectives:

- Management accountants as the function in scope
- Enablers of change in the management accounting function (e.g., IT function)
- Decision-makers and internal customers (e.g., sales managers and production managers)

4.3.4 Evolution of the Interview Process

As previously mentioned, the research was conducted through an iterative process. As shown in Fig. 4.1, the information and knowledge gained in one interview were used for the preparation of the next interview. The interview process was reviewed after each interview. Particularly after the first few interviews and preliminary phone sessions, the learnings were incorporated into the guidelines and structure of the remaining interviews. For instance, the order of topics was adjusted. Based on the integration of a review of potentially relevant theories, one focus of the interviews was on the motivation and reasoning behind implementing digitization tools and projects to be able to better relate it back to the theory. In this context, detailed questions regarding the motivation for actions and reasoning were added.

The different backgrounds, experience, and roles of the interviewees were taken into account when timing the interviews and setting the potential focus topics. For instance, the interview with an employee who was part of a big data project in management accounting focused (time-wise) more on questions on tools than the interview with the HR representative who could provide further information on the skills and backgrounds needed in management accounting in the future. Due to the limited amount of time available for each interview, questions that were not leading to relevant findings were omitted to allow additional time for more relevant topics (especially in the later stage with regard to questions relevant for theory development).

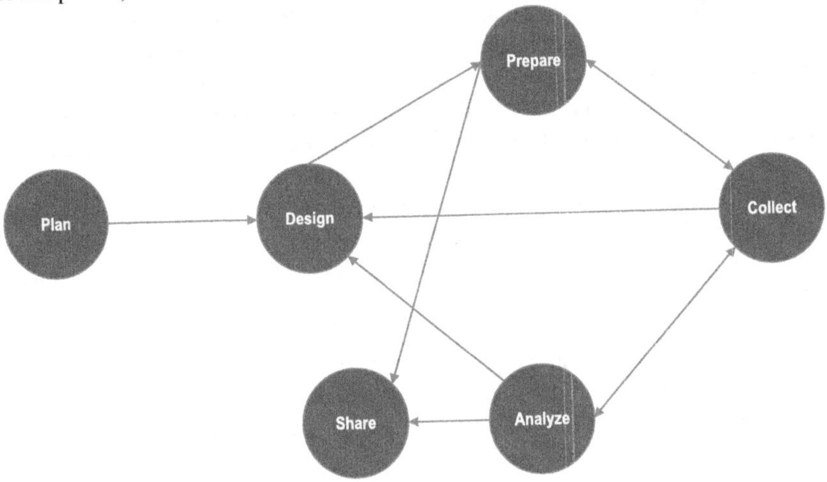

Fig. 4.1 Iterative research process. (Based on Yin, 2009)

4.4 Case Companies

Five companies were involved in this qualitative case study (see Fig. 4.2). As previously described, all five companies fulfilled the specified selection criteria and were showing their willingness to be part of research study. Their interest in the topic and their willingness to share and to learn from other companies was the main driver of their agreement to participate.

In this section, the main characteristics of the companies are described, followed by the findings with regard to the impact of digitization on the management accounting function. The cases are presented based on the chronological order of the preliminary interviews. One major condition for the companies to participate was their permission to use the results anonymously. Hence, the description of the cases remains on a level that does not allow the specific company to be identified.

	Case 1	Case 2	Case 3	Case 4	Case 5
Revenues [bn EUR]	20–50	1-10	1-10	1-10	20–50
Employees ['000]	> 100	> 10-20	>10-20	>10-20	>100
Industry	Pharma & Chemicals	Consumer Goods	Consumer Goods	Mechanical Engineering	Automotive supplier
Interviews [#]	4	3	7	4	3

Fig. 4.2 Overview of case companies

4.5 Interviews

4.5.1 Empirical Research Process

To gain useful empirical insights, a structured research process was followed. The process comprised six steps for each case company, as described next. The first three steps were conducted in parallel for the majority of the cases to ensure a relevant set of companies and interviewees, whereas the main interviews were conducted sequentially.

4.5.1.1 Establish Contacts

The first step of the research process was to identify and gain access to contacts. Several sources for contacts were considered. In addition to those from prior studies and activities, contacts were identified through conventions for management accounting professionals and professional social networks. The goal was to connect with the management accounting departments in companies that meet the selection criteria. Based on the discussions and interviews with the employees from the management accounting function, other interviews (with internal customers and enablers) were triggered, with the management accounting interviewee as the main contact person. The logic behind this approach was that the management accounting employees were interested in participating because they could learn from the feedback and results.

4.5.1.2 Raise Interest

The second step involved raising interest not only in the topic but also in participating in the study, which is an investment of time. Hence, a document was prepared and shared with the selected contacts that introduced the researcher and the research questions. Preliminary interviews were then organized via email or the messaging functions of professional social networks (e.g., LinkedIn).

4.5.1.3 Conduct Preliminary Interviews

The preliminary interviews were conducted by the researcher with the contacts in the management accounting departments of each case company. The preliminary interviews lasted between 30 and 75 min. and mainly covered four topics.

First, the interviewee was asked to introduce himself and his position and tasks. Second, the interviewee described the overall structure of the company, especially with regard to the management accounting function. This topic varied in terms of time spent because the researcher had a good understanding of some of the companies from desk research (publicly available information) and from prior business activities.

Third, the research framework and the research questions of the study were described by the researcher and then discussed with regard to their relevance to the respective company. The high-level discussion of the questions was crucial to determine if the questions are of relevance to management accounting professionals because the aim of this study is to provide findings that are important for both researchers and practitioners. Another goal of the discussion was to detect whether the company could add considerable insights to the findings of the study.

Fourth, the methodology, especially with regard to the empirical research process, was explained by the researcher. One focus of this part was to stress the importance of triangulation on this topic (the goal of conducting interviews with several stakeholders). Finally, the immediate next steps were outlined in terms of organizing the interview days and providing feedback from the preliminary interviews.

4.5.1.4 Feedback Document and Setup of Interview Days

After conducting all preliminary interviews, the findings were analyzed and summarized to further specify the interview guidelines. Additionally, a selection of findings was provided to the participants as the first round of feedback to maintain their interest for the upcoming interviews. When providing the feedback document, the contact person also received a suggested agenda for the interview day at the company premises. The management accounting interviewees were also asked to share the document with their colleagues in HR, IT, sales, and production to explain the procedure for the interview day and as a basis to arrange time slots for interviews.

4.5.1.5 Interview Days

The interviews were conducted in person and at the premises of the companies for a number of reasons. First, it reduces the commitment that the participants must make in terms of time (compared to meeting at another place). Additionally, it is advantageous to discuss the questions in the natural surroundings of the employees. It also allows the researcher to obtain further insights into topics discussed during the interview; for example, if a new tool was introduced, the participants could demonstrate the tool or share the results of the tool's analyses. The same applies to documents (e.g., presentations and reports) that were discussed during the interviews. Because the documents may be partially confidential, participants might not be willing to share (in terms of sending out via email) certain documents with outsiders. However, the in-person discussion and viewing of these documents and tools allow the researcher to gain further insights and impressions while at the same time protecting the participant from risk. The researcher can also obtain additional insights from the body language of the participants, which can provide important cues that the spoken word (via the telephone) may not reveal.

Furthermore, more people (e.g., from the management accounting teams) attended the meetings on the actual interview days, which showed that there was wider interest within the companies. Hence, there were not just one-on-one interviews but also group discussions, indicating that even within single companies, there are multiple viewpoints on how digitization impacts management accounting and on how a company should approach the topic. Apart from the additional discussions and talks that happened spontaneously, interviews with 3–4 stakeholders were conducted at each company. These interviews lasted between approximately 30 and 120 min. each. All participants agreed to the request for audio recordings of the interviews, enabling the researcher to focus on the content rather than on taking notes. Most of the interviews were conducted in German because the participants were largely based in German-speaking countries. Figure 4.3 provides a model agenda for an interview day.

Topic	Participants	Approx. duration
Introduction and admin	Researcher and management accountant	15–30 min
Interview with enabler IT	Researcher and employee from IT department	30–60 min
Interview with internal customer	Researcher and Internal customer (e.g., from sales or manufacturing)	30–60 min
Interview with enabler HR	Researcher and employee from HR department	30–60 min
Interview with management accountant	Researcher and management accountant	30–90 min
Wrap-up	Researcher and management accountant	15 30 min

Fig. 4.3 Exemplary agenda for interview da at case companies

4.5.1.6 Feedback Loop

As previously mentioned, the empirical research followed an iterative process. After each interview day, the interviews were transcribed and analyzed to include the findings and learnings in the next interview. After the interviews were conducted, interviewees were (based on availability) invited to discuss the findings. The reason to do so was to ensure that statements and opinions were understood correctly. Figure 4.4 shows an overview of the empirical research process that was defined and conducted for this study.

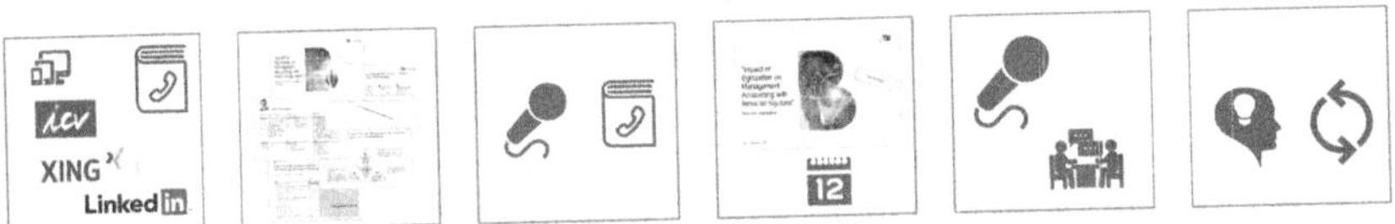

Establish contacts
> Leverage personal contacts
> Visit fairs and events to build up contacts
> Cold-calling and cold-messaging via professional social networks (LinkedIn/Xing)

Raise interest
> Prepare document to introduce researcher (CV) and research topic
> Provide document to contacts who have agreed on phone call

Conduct preliminary interviews
> Introduce research topic & researcher
> (If new contact) introduce contact & company
> Discuss research questions and relevant aspects
> Methodology & next steps

Provide feedback and set up interview days
> Summary of preliminary interview findings
> Information on literature findings
> (Suggested) agenda for interview day
> Development/adjustment of interview guideline

Conduct interview days
> Interviews with 3-4 stake holders at the premises of the company
> Aim for interviews of 1–1.5 hours each
> Discussion/'trial' of relevant documents/tools
> Recording of interviews

Provide feedback
> Summarize findings from interviews in comprehensive but interesting format (sanitized)
> If participants are interested, provide document to participants discuss findings over the phone

Fig. 4.4 Empirical research process

4.5.2 Interviews with Management Accountants

As described in Fig. 4.5, three major perspectives on the impact of digitization on management accounting within the companies were examined: those of the management accountants, enablers, and internal customers. The only perspective included in the preliminary interviews was of employees from the management accounting function. Based on those initial conversations, the researcher discussed the research questions in deeper detail along with additional findings from the other perspectives in subsequent interviews. All three interviewee types were not only questioned on what changes and impact they have experienced from digitization but also what they expect to see in the future.

Based on the perspective of the interviewee, the focus of the questions differed. For example, when speaking to interviewees with the enabler perspective (e.g., from the IT and HR departments), the focus of the questions was on the tools and systems in management accounting and on the skills of management accountants, respectively. The focus of interviews with decision-makers was on questions regarding their expectations of the service provided by management accountants and other topics found in the interview guidelines in the appendix. However, the depth of the discussions was different from those with management accountants. In the interviews with management accountants, all four research questions were broached. Because the management accountants have the deepest knowledge in the field, the interviews also were the longest in terms of minutes (see Fig. 4.5).

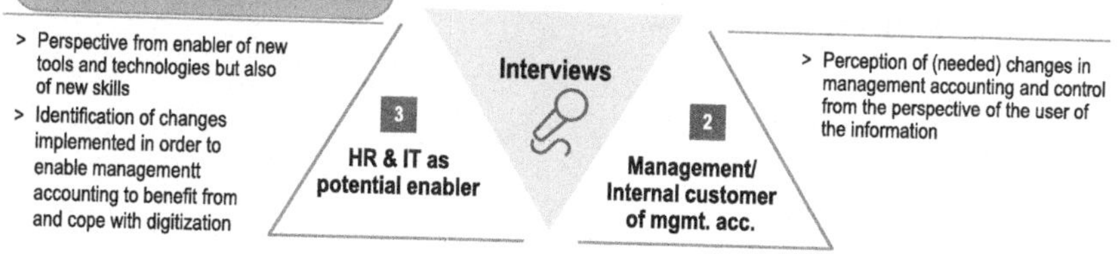

Fig. 4.5 Interview perspectives covered (Lachmann & Holtkemper, 2021)

4.5.3 Interviews with Decision-Makers

The decision-makers of each company were interviewed to reflect the perspective of managers in sales, production, or research and development (R&D) who depend on the management accountants' information to make decisions. These internal customers (customers in terms of receiving information and advice from the management accountants) range from sales managers to heads of manufacturing to engineers in the R&D function of the case companies. To reflect a broad range of perspectives, the participant from the internal customer perspective varied among the case companies. All three internal customer perspectives (sales, production, and R&D) were not covered for each case due to the limited capacities of the participating companies. The aim was to cover at least one internal customer in detail rather than merely scratching the surface with several internal customers.

4.5.4 Interviews with Management Accounting Enablers

The third perspective is that of the enablers, which was represented by employees from the HR and IT functions because these two functions are key enablers of change with regard to employee skills and backgrounds as well as the technology applied in the management accounting function.

With regard to HR, the knowledge and skills necessary in times of management accounting digitization were examined. The perspective covers the proactive development of current employees (e.g., training on the job or seminars), as well as the recruiting of new personnel with the knowledge and skills needed in management accounting.

As previously mentioned, 28 interviews were conducted with participants from all perspectives. Figure 4.6 describes the position of each interviewee, the perspective covered, the respective case company, and the duration of each interview.

Figure 4.7 shows the distribution of the 28 interviews along the case companies and the additional expert interviews.

#	Position	Perspective	Case, category	Duration (in min)
1	Head of Corporate Business Intelligence	Management Accounting & IT/BI	Company 1	121
2	In-house Consultant Controlling Business Software	Management Accounting & Process Optimization	Company 1	60
3	HR Global Business Partner Controlling & Accounting Operations	Human Resources	Company 1	60
4	Head of Balance Sheet and Cash Flow Controlling	Management Accounting & Finance	Company 1	60
5	Manager Revenue Controlling	Management Accounting	Company 2	64
6	Key Account Manager	Internal customer	Company 2	22
7	Associated Director - Integrated Business Planning	IT	Company 2	46
8	Customer Director (Sales)	Internal customer	Company 3	43
9	Analytic Expert in Controlling	Management Accounting	Company 3	55
10	Head of Financial Analytics/Reporting	Management Accounting	Company 3	30
11	Head of Controlling Europe	Management Accounting	Company 3	27
12	IT Expert	IT	Company 3	54
13	Controller with focus on Planning and Reporting	Management Accounting	Company 3	21
14	Head of Finance Academy	HR	Company 3	38
15	Business-Process Manager im Bereich Finance und Controlling	IT/Business Process Management	Company 4	38
16	Head of Project Management Office IT	IT Project Planing	Company 4	26
17	Vice President Global Engineering	Customer (Engineering)	Company 4	27
18	Vice President Management Accounting Digital Division	Management Accounting	Company 4	40
19	Head of Manufacturing Controlling Division One	Managment Accounting & IT	Company 5	123
20	HR Business Partner for Finance and Controlling	Human Resources	Company 5	63
21	Co-Head of F&E for Division One	Internal Customer	Company 5	59
22	Director Controlling	Management Accounting Expert	Chemicals company	120
23	Head of Shared Service Center	Management Accounting Expert	Consumer Goods Company	60
24	CEO & Founder	Management Accounting Software	Software Provider	58
25	CEO & Founder	Management Accounting Software	Software Provider	53
26	Director Southern Europe, Finance Partner for Sales & Marketing	Management Accounting Software	Software Provider	50
27	CFO Advisory Consultant	Management Accounting Software	Software Provider	67
28	Professor for Controlling/Management Accounting	Management Accounting Expert	University	60

Fig. 4.6 Interviewees

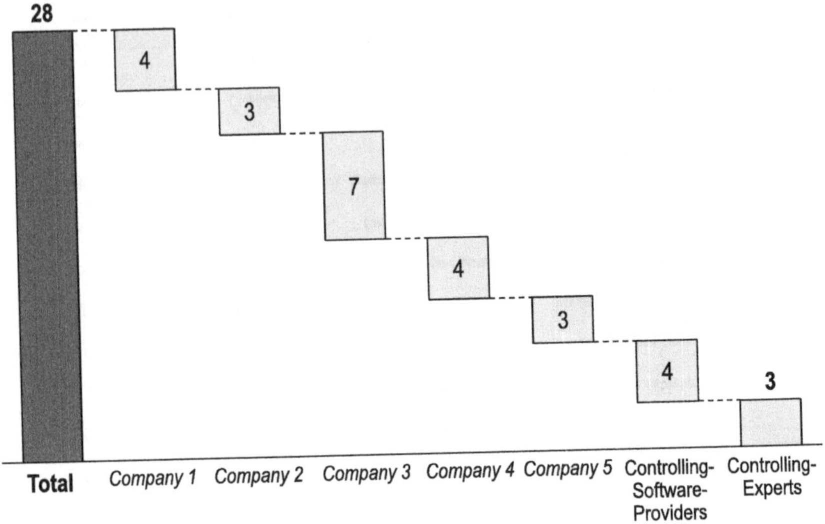

Fig. 4.7 Interviews by company, category

4.6 Analysis of Interviews: Coding Methodology

For the analysis of the data, the author worked with MAXQDA, which is a program for text analysis. MAXQDA facilitates a systematic text analysis by providing a hierarchical code system. This code system converts the data into a tree structure. Through the assignment of codes to relevant text segments, it is possible to retrieve thematically significant sections of text (Kuckartz et al., 2007). For the documentation of analytical ideas and for support during the course of the study, the author created memos. For example, the author wrote code comments to record the basic assumption that stands behind the respective codes.

Three levels of coding were conducted and prepared based on Strauss and Corbin (1998). The first level was open coding: data is "fractured" (e.g., into lines or sentences), and events are given conceptual labels and are grouped into categories and subcategories. During the analyses, the author moved gradually from first-order categories to analytical, second-order categories to overarching themes and dimensions. For example, open coding was applied to link answers to one of the research questions. If, for instance, an interviewee talked about skills required, a certain code was applied. Additionally, the answers for each research question were further differentiated by applying more detailed codes (second order). For instance, answers indicating the importance of IT skills were marked with the same code to be able to compare and group the answers. The open coding was also applied to the way the companies implement digitization in management accounting. Answers indicating a measure with a cost focus were, for instance, marked with a specific code.

Based on the open coding, axial coding was conducted. Axial coding categories are "related to their properties, and relationships among categories (provisional propositions) are tested against additional data" (Strauss & Corbin, 1990, p. 13). In this step, relationships between answers to different research questions were coded. This helped to categorize and derive the archetypes described later in this study. For deriving the archetypes, selective coding was applied. This refers to the approach in which "all categories are integrated around a 'core' category, and categories that need further explication are filled-in with descriptive detail or dropped" (Strauss & Corbin, 1990, p. 14). For this study, selective coding was crucial because a vast amount of data was gathered. To identify the important relationships and to derive the framework, codes and information having low or no explanatory power were dropped for the research questions. Figure 4.8 shows examples of the codes applied.

#	Statement/ quote	Example codes	Relevant research question
1	"Whereas nowadays, still quite a lot of resources are needed for reporting, in the future, the management accountant will focus on more value-creating tasks in giving advice to decision-makers. A report that took me several hours in the past can be created automatically out of the ERP system", Management Accountant, Company 3.	- old tasks - new tasks - new tools - resources/headcount - management accountant perspective	RQ1, RQ2a
2	"[A]automation in the execution of tasks will increase further. Tasks that are today conducted by colleagues in management accounting, [such as] creating reports, is already and will be further executed automatically", IT Manager, Company 2.	- old tasks - automation - IT perspective	RQ1
3	We are convinced that by automation and use of synergies, we will be able to provide the same level of service with fewer employees because ... there will be less manual work needed. Of course, this should also allow us to reduce personnel costs in the management accounting teams" (Head of Corporate Business Intelligence, Company 1).	- automation - personnel cost reduction - manual work reduction - resources/headcount	RQ1, RQ2a
4	**We have a finance academy that [offers] business** partner skill seminars, where top management is on-site and the controllers are given training on the new role. You do case studies there and you just have very open discussions" (HR Business Partner, Company 1).	- training - new role - education - skills	RQ3
5	"The top management in the headquarters appreciated our effort in big data and, in the beginning, they were fascinated by [the] machine learning and data science that we suggested and implemented. However, because we are a listed company and **need to provide financial results every quarter, ...** management wanted to see results in terms of revenue growth ... Hence, further investments were postponed" (Management Accountant, Company 2).	- change approach - big data - new teams - organizational change - motivation - performance measurement **- financial impact** - management accountant perspective	RQ3

Fig. 4.8 Example codes

#	Statement/ quote	Example codes	Relevant research question
6	"[W]e gather a lot of data and some data we even buy. However, I think we can and have to improve further in making use of that data. When I'm sitting with a client in a meeting, I need to have the information available in a nice and presentable format. I don't want to sit there and scroll through a large Excel file" (Key Account Manager, Company 2).	- internal customer perspective - client needs - new tasks - data	RQ1
7	"I think it cannot be done without sound finance and accounting knowledge. This is and will be the base of our work. If someone understands how [to] approach a complex problem [and] who … to contact for expertise, if somebody brings that, then, somehow, he also gets mass data right", (Management Accountant, Company 2).	- skills - educational background - accounting knowhow - problem solving	RQ3
8	"I am actually looking forward to further automation because the work that can be done by machines is repetitive and, hence, rather boring for me. I can then focus on solving more challenges and problems and apply new technologies, [such as] analysing new data pools with the help of neural networks" (Management Accountant, Company 3).	- motivation - change approach - new tasks - old tasks - management accountant perspective	RQ1, RQ2a
9	"In terms of training and education, I think we still need a mix of methods because different people learn differently and different contents are taught better in different ways. When it comes to content, I really think we should update and improve our training … to keep up with the challenges and developments we face in management accounting but also in other functions" (HR Business Partner, Company 5).	- skills - educational background - HR perspective	RQ3
10	"I am a big supporter of my team members who drive new initiatives and bring up ideas to use data. However, we always try to analyse only data for specific questions we try to answer. We don't want to analyse random data into the blue just for the purpose of doing 'big data'. What we are trying to do is to use new technologies and skills but still … be efficient in the way we work" (Manager, Controlling, Company 5)	- management accountant perspective - change approach - big data - data analytics - new tasks	RQ1, RQ2, RQ3

Fig. 4.8 (continued)

5 Findings

The findings section of this dissertation is structured as follows. In the first subsection (5.1), the findings regarding the first three research questions are described and analyzed for each of the five cases. Based on the findings from each case, the differences and similarities between the cases are analyzed (subsections 5.2–5.4) and two archetypes are derived (subsection 5.5). These two archetypes are then discussed, and the five cases are categorized (subsection 5.6–5.7). Additionally, the perspective of software providers on the subject is described (subsection 5.8).

5.1 Five Cases of Digitization in Management Accounting

5.1.1 Case 1: Pharma and Chemicals Conglomerate

Company 1 is a large pharmaceutical and chemicals conglomerate with more than 100,000 employees and over 40 billion euros in revenue. The company is publicly listed on the stock exchange. Four interviews were conducted within the company. The interviews covered three perspectives: those of the management accounting employee and management accounting manager (head of BI section within management accounting), in-house consultant driving digitization projects, and the supporting function (HR partner for the finance and accounting function).

5.1.1.1 Overview: Cost Reduction in Focus

Company 1 focuses its digitization efforts of the management accounting function on streamlining it with the main objective to increase efficiency. With the help of digitization, it is expected that the tasks of management accounting will be conducted

O. Holtkemper, *Digitization of the Management Accounting Function*, Controlling und Rechnungslegung – Managerial and Financial Accounting, https://doi.org/10.1007/978-3-658-31509-2_5

faster with fewer resources and higher reliability. The change is driven top-down by senior management to achieve ambitious cost-reduction targets for the whole company. The overall target is broken down and given to each function as a savings target. In management accounting, process automation and standardization are seen as key methods to achieve cost-reduction goals, especially in reporting. The reorganization efforts of Company 1 have been pushed further by the planned merger with another company. With the help of digitization, synergies and cost reductions are goals in merging two efficient companies.

5.1.1.2 Findings RQ1: Impact of Digitization on Tasks and Tools of Management Accounting

Management accounting at Company 1 has transformed into a role that has increased its focus on advisory tasks. The idea is to have management accountants concentrate their time and efforts on decision support, with the help of specialist teams that will focus on data analytics and providing tools to the management accountants. In the future, Company 1 is expected to be able to bundle even more tasks in shared service centers. Based on their standardized processes, the automation of processes is expected to be further driven. In addition to focusing on management accounting advising, local management accountants will also cover related tasks such as finance and accounting advising: "*[Although] we have a number of specialist employees in local teams today, in the future, fewer employees will cover the advisory role for finance, management accounting, and tax*" (HR Business Partner, Company 1).

The reasoning behind the business partner role covering several disciplines is that the manual tasks for the preparation of reports or analyses of data will be either further automated or conducted in centralized teams. The business partners can, therefore, dedicate themselves to the advisory task. One major focus of Company 1 is the inclusion of more data and (big data) analytics into standard reporting. Currently, the focus is on financial and accounting data. However, in the long run, further information relevant for important business decisions is to be included. To do so, there is a plan to connect various data pools from different functions. The overall goal is to add more meaning to the data that has been gathered by different functions by rolling out standardized practices in terms of data analysis. This will not only improve data quality and comparability but also the ability to automate. Standardization is carried out within the divisions of Company 1 regarding the ERP solutions used but will expand to other areas in the near future.

A new reporting solution in a dashboard format has recently been introduced in Company 1. It allows managers to view the division, region, and unit they are working in and is an efficient way of drilling into financial data and figuring out the origin of effects on, for instance, revenues. The main objective of the new tool and the consolidation of the data sources behind the system is to have a single main source of information. Whereas in the past, discussions were often started with numbers from different sources, "*discussions with one source of truth lead to the content right away*" (Head of Corporate Business Intelligence, Company 1). Additionally, the tool can be used as a communication and cooperation platform.

5.1.1.3 Findings RQ2: Impact of Digitization on Organizational and Geographical Setup of Management Accounting, Drivers and Barriers of Digitization in Management Accounting

In the current reorganization process, the organizational structure of Company 1 has been streamlined. Previously, it was a holding organization with divisions that were autonomous. The major corporate functions are being synergized so there is only one source for each function across the divisions. This is because there was a management accounting function for each of the divisions and all were able to make policies and governance and define their own processes. An interviewee from Company 1 argues that "*so much diversity is not due to the business models but the complexity of the organizational structure and, therefore, it has been decided that there should be only each function only once*" (Head of Corporate Business Intelligence, Company 1). Hence, there is now only one management accounting function.

In the process of reorganizing and building the new organizational structure, for management accounting, digitization plays an important role in realizing synergies and effects that the company has targeted. The change is being introduced in a "soft" rather than hard approach; in other words, the new processes are rolled out step by step and not all at once in a disruptive manner: "*We are aiming at not risking the operational business. That's why we conduct the change step by step. Also, we are able to analyze the change and impact better when we do it in a soft change approach*" (In-house Consultant Controlling Business Software, Company 1).

From an organizational point of view, shared service centers are vital for Company 1. Nevertheless, the focus is only on highly repetitive and non-complex tasks, such as simple accounting tasks rather than management accounting tasks. One difficulty mentioned with regard to shared service centers is the fluctuation of employees, which is much higher than in other units.

In addition to the restructuring of the existing functions, new teams have been formed for data analytics. New data scientist roles have been established, which work closely with and support management accounting in applying new analytical tools. Automation and use of synergies are expected to reduce the number of management accountants across the organization, especially in the local division units, where they will be leveraged to decrease personnel costs: "*We are convinced that by automation and use of synergies, we will be able to provide the same level of service with fewer employees because … there will be less manual work needed. Of course, this should also allow us to reduce personnel costs in the management accounting teams*" (Head of Corporate Business Intelligence, Company 1).

When discussing barriers and drivers of digitization, the varying motivations of the different functions and employees stood out when speaking to interviewees. Company 1 has taken the measures mainly to reduce costs and has prescribed goals that must be met. Additionally, in-house consulting units have been involved to drive change from a neutral point of view. The pressure to improve is high due to a planned merger with another company. Employees at Company 1 expect the newly acquired company to be strong in the digitalization of their function and, hence, feel pressure to improve to be able to contend in an internally competitive environment where functions are being merged in the future: "*When merging the two companies, we will try to benefit from the strength of both companies. We will be able to benefit from the progress the other company has made in terms of digitization of its business model but also of its internal processes*" (Head of Balance Sheet and Cashflow Controlling, Company 1). However, as mentioned, each division's management accounting function had previously built up its own processes, structures, and IT landscape. Hence, the complexity and potential risk of disturbing the operational business was described as a barrier to change.

5.1.1.4 Findings RQ3: Impact of Digitization on Educational Backgrounds and Skills in Management Accounting

In Company 1, the required skill sets for management accountants are currently being developed by HR. However, because tasks are not yet clearly defined, it is difficult to specify the skills needed, although management accountants and HR staff are aware of the future need for different skill sets. The new advisory role will require strong knowledge of the business and good communication skills from the management accountants, in addition to proficiency with statistics and finance/accounting. Management accountants are also expected to have a basic understanding of new technologies and must be able to interpret the findings from data analytics.

Training programs and curricula are also being further developed at Company 1. There is a "*finance academy that [offers] business partner skill seminars, where top management is on-site and the controllers are given training on the new role. You do case studies there and you just have very open discussions*" (HR Business Partner, Company 1).

One major challenge is to develop people who are strong at preparing data toward a role in which they focus on interpreting data and setting it into context to solve business problems and support decision-making: "*To develop these employees toward a business partner role is a challenge. Business partners will be expected to inhibit a skill set that is much broader than those of management accountants in the past. There will be a need for employees who not only understand the pharma and chemicals business, finance, and accounting but also [are] able to deal with data and technologies*" (HR Business Partner, Company 1). Under digitization, the tasks of collecting and preparing data will either be conducted by machines or transferred to shared service centers. In addition to classroom training, there is on-the-job training conducted to convey skills. Based on specific demands from management, the management accountant needs to adapt and learn, such as from more experienced colleagues. This option to learn from colleagues proves more difficult in times of digitization because the more experienced colleagues need to adapt, as well.

5.1.2 Case 2: Beverage Manufacturer

5.1.2.1 Introduction to Company

Company 2 is considered one of the world's largest beverage companies and is headquartered in the United States. Their European subsidiary employs around 10,000 people and generates around EUR 10 billion. The company is publicly listed on the stock exchange. Three interviews were arranged with employees from the European subsidiary of the global conglomerate and covered the perspectives of management accounting, a supporting function (IT), and an internal customer (key account management).

5.1.2.2 Overview: Shifting from Bottom-up Toward Top-Down Focus

Company 2's digitization efforts in management accounting have focused on measures that were driven bottom-up by the management accountants themselves. However, there has recently been a shift in terms of the digitization strategy toward an increase in efficiency by optimizing the way traditional management accounting tasks are conducted: "*The top management in the headquarters appreciated our effort in big data and, in the beginning, they were fascinated by [the] machine learning and data science that we suggested and implemented. However, because we are a listed company and need to provide financial results every quarter, ... management wanted to see results in terms of revenue growth... Hence, further investments were postponed*" (Management Accountant, Company 2).

5.1.2.3 Findings RQ1

Based on initiatives from the management accounting team, new tasks and roles were introduced with a focus on analyzing more data sources and harvesting the existing data more efficiently. The aim was to identify and realize further revenue potential (e.g., by defining measures in terms of pricing or on improving certain sales channels). The intention was to justify operative and strategic decisions with facts and data rather than gut feeling. The company recently formed a big data team within management accounting but it was not able to meet the ambitious targets with regard to identifying additional revenue potential, which has resulted in the shift back toward conducting work more efficiently rather than developing new and sophisticated data models that may not necessarily lead to increasing revenues: "*We decreased the size of the team and went back to old structures*" (Head of Financial Analytics/Reporting, Company 2). The focus of management accounting is now back to working efficiently and fulfilling business needs.

However, with regard to the tasks of management accounting for Company 2, a shift from repetitive reporting and planning tasks toward more dynamic support of sales and other functions is in progress. Company 2 aims to further adapt management accounting to the fast-moving character of the consumer goods business with the help of digitization. Hence, the role of management accounting is changing, as more data must be analyzed and used to support decisions in the field. In addition to the data analytics aspect, the focus is increasingly on the advisory aspect of the functions: "*We are in fast-moving consumer goods. With the help of digitization, we have to be able to make faster and better decisions based on facts. Management accounting should be able to support managers' decisions better and faster in the future*" (Manager, Management Accounting, Company 2). With regard to new tools and systems, Company 2 has recently invested in upgrading ERP systems and the software landscape. Because Company 2 is the market leader in a diminishing market, the need for new revenue potential has encouraged measures to improve sales in the field. Improving the execution in the field has been a major focus; as such, measures were derived to support the sales representatives with better data from management accounting.

With the help of management accounting and IT, new KPIs to measure and raise execution standards were introduced. A new app was developed that sales representatives can open on their tablets to review real-time data from the ERP system and to gather data at the client's premises, such as the extent to which marketing measures have been implemented and the kinds of products the clients have on their shelves.

Another recent focus has been to improve the visualization of (financial) data: "*[W]e gather a lot of data and some data we even buy. However, I think we can and have to improve further in making use of that data. When I'm sitting with a client in a meeting, I need to have the information available in a nice and presentable format. I don't want to sit there and scroll through a large Excel file*" (Key Account Manager, Company 2). In addition to execution, optimizing operational processes and improving short-term sales measures with the use of data have also been key strategies. Discounts, marketing measures, and offers are to be further optimized with timely data (i.e., real-time or a maximum of 24 h' old), which will have a significant impact on planning and budgeting and shorten the cycles to benefit from this up-to-date data: "*[W]e need to improve the collaboration between the technical site, which knows what is possible, and the business site. Management accounting sits at that interface and needs to [bridge] that gap*" (IT Manager, Company 2).

5.1.2.4 Findings RQ2

With regard to the impact on the organizational setup of management accounting, Company 2 has focused on several recent issues. New teams were formed for pilot projects to deal with topics related to digitization. However, as previously mentioned, the team focusing on big data was not able to meet the ambitious targets with regard to additional revenue potential: "*[F]or two years, we had a team, which was actually focusing on big data analytics. The job was very simple—increasing our sales by as much as x percent through projects in the big data area. Unfortunately, the team was then dissolved again because the goals were not achieved*" (Management Accountant, Company 2). Shared service centers were established but the previous goals were not heavily focused on cost. The recent shift toward cost efficiency is expected to cause more (management) accounting tasks to be performed within shared service centers. Thus far, mainly basic accounting tasks have been transferred to shared service centers, such as the booking of accounting documents. The reporting function is also located in the shared service center: "*Reporting should now also be standardized. Currently, for instance, each country has its own reporting world. ... [T]o automate further, we need to improve on this*" (IT Manager, Company 2). Another challenging aspect for Company 2 is that different departments work on data mining and digitization projects in various functions and regions. The goal is to bundle the efforts and expertise for maximum benefit. To increase the comparability of KPIs and the usability of data in general, serious efforts need to be made to harmonize the standards further across divisions and functions.

5.1.2.5 Findings RQ3

Company 2 is following an approach to establish experts with data analytics skills while increasing the overall level of IT and statistics knowledge among all management accountants simultaneously. Team managers try to level the skill sets within their teams. However, no specific adjustments for training and recruiting have been made so far, but the necessity to incorporate new concepts and content in terms of training and recruiting requirements has been recognized. Nevertheless, HR and management have not yet been able to provide further guidance: "*All the effort to improve our skills and adjust requirements have been driven by us in management accounting. HR has not provided any guidance or concepts on how to prepare our employees for digitization. I think this is where we can improve our efforts*" (Team Lead, Management Accounting, Company 2). As the company is becoming more cost-sensitive, training has become a matter that will only be focused on when the budget is available.

With regard to skills needed in times of digitization, the discussions suggest that basic finance and accounting knowledge are still essential for management accountants: "*I think it cannot be done without sound finance and accounting knowledge. This is and will be the base of our work*" (Management Accountant, Company 2). Also, general problem-solving skills will still be of high importance: "*If someone understands how [to] approach a complex problem [and] who … to contact for expertise, if somebody brings that, then, somehow, he also gets mass data right*" (Management Accountant, Company 2).

5.1.3 Case 3: Consumer Goods Company

5.1.3.1 Introduction to Company

Company 3 is a publicly listed European consumer goods company with an international footprint in the United States and Asia. The company has around 20,000 employees globally and revenues that amount to approximately 7 billion euros. Seven interviews were conducted with various personnel at the company, covering the management accounting (expert role, manager, and CFO of one region), supporting function (HR and IT), and internal customer (sales manager) perspectives.

5.1.3.2 Overview: Bottom-up Initiatives Driven by Management Accounting Teams

Company 3 applies a digitization approach that is primarily driven by initiatives and ideas from management accountants. New tools are being tested and introduced by a management accounting team to enhance the value-add of reporting and planning, which includes providing extra information that the stakeholders would not have otherwise. The trigger for new tools can come from various sources, including local management accountants, internal customer needs, or even a colleague in

IT who discovers a new tool provided by a software supplier that the company is closely related to. Additionally, new roles and experts have been introduced to further explore innovative technologies such as artificial intelligence to assist with management accounting tasks.

With regard to data, Company 3 focuses on making data that is currently available usable: "*We have enough data to meet all our tasks; however, the data is often either unstructured or we don't know how to connect different datasets. For us, this is clearly not just an IT challenge but also a task for management accountants because they know the processes behind the data and know how they relate*" (Customer Director, Company 3). To channel the innovation within management accounting, a central management accounting team is gathering ideas from local teams and developing solutions to distribute them throughout the whole organization. The aim is to drive innovation and, at the same time, ensure standardization across functions to maintain the comparability of data, analyses, and systems between different entities, business units, and geographies within the company.

5.1.3.3 Findings RQ1

Management accounting needs to ensure that it adds value in times of increasing complexity through providing insights, knowledge, and support to other functions: "*It always comes down to adding value to the business, and the complexity of our business is [growing]. That is why, if we do not use technology, we won't be able to solve the issues for the business and, hence, will no longer add substantial value to the company*" (Management Accountant, Company 3). Overall, Company 3 aims to keep track with technological developments.

With regard to reporting, Company 3 aims toward more flexible self-service reporting: "*I think our reporting is already good but it needs to go one step further, namely in the field of self-service reporting. It will allow people to pull their own reports and data based on their needs. Especially for more complex requests, it will be relevant because those questions cannot be answered by standard reports but must be answered flexibly from within the system*" (Management Accountant, Company 3). With self-service reporting via dashboards and a higher degree of reporting automation, the role of management accountants will change to that of a business partner who advises management based on the understanding of (financial) data and the business.

Management accounting in Company 3 focuses on three major aspects to preserve its relevance to the business and to continue adding value as an internal service provider: "*One of the aims is to be the obvious standard-setter when it comes to formats, KPIs, processes, and tools. Another one is to further build analytical expertise. Finally, we need to be driving innovation in our field of expertise to stay ahead of the game and ... to be valuable as a business partner*" (Team Lead, Management Accounting, Company 3). Digitization and innovation are mainly driven by the ideas of the management accountants. Little guidance is provided top-down by management: "*An overall vision of the future for finance and accounting would be helpful as guidance but does not exist in detail.... For us, digitization is rather driven out of the teams and by ideas of employees*" (Management Accountant, Company 3). Another theme that stands out from the discussions with Company 3 interviewees is the positive attitude toward digitization. Management accountants approach and drive the changes with an optimistic attitude and focus on the benefits: "*I am actually looking forward to further automation because the work that can be done by machines is repetitive and, hence, rather boring for me. I can then focus on solving more challenges and problems and apply new technologies, [such as] analyzing new data pools with the help of neural networks*" (Management Accountant, Company 3).

5.1.3.4 Findings RQ2

As mentioned earlier, a centralized team of management accountants, gathering ideas on new methods from within the organization, has been established to drive digitization. Most ideas have been brought up by the local management accountants and then managed and shared by a central team to allow for global use and ensure standards across the organization. Company 3 currently uses shared service centers to only a very limited extent in management accounting. The primary aim is not to save costs but to ensure standardization, which is demonstrated by the company's strategy to open the shared service center in a high-cost rather than low-cost country. One reason for Company 3 to focus on innovation and less on cost-reduction measures is the strong position of the workers' council, which curbs more radical measures. Another barrier is the "*silo mentality that many conglomerates with several divisions encounter. Everyone is trying to get the best for his division or function*" (Management Accountant, Company 3). When investments are considered for new software and tools, the aim is mainly to improve decision-making and, hence, the arguments in favor of investments are mostly strategic: "*Generally, the idea is to start small but think big, [such as] introducing something new for a small unit but having in mind the potential rollout for the whole organization*" (Management Accounting Team Lead, Company 3).

5.1.3.5 Findings RQ3

According to Company 3, basic data literacy is and will be even more crucial for every management accountant in the future. However, the basis should still be deep finance and accounting knowledge. Initial ideas for training specifically for digitization have been discussed and mainly initiated by management accountants. Thus far, little support from the central HR function has been received, and management accountants complain about the lack of concrete efforts from HR on preparing employees for digitization. Currently, major initiatives for training in management accounting are originated from the teams and single employees: "*When I want to improve on a certain topic like coding or even accounting standards, my own initiative is required to a large extent ... to be able to attend training or get training material*" (Management Accountant, Company 3). Another interviewee states: "*Human resources is not pushing for change and for [the] development of the employees. Initiatives come from the teams and employees, rather than top-down from management and HR*" (Management Accounting Team Lead, Company 3).

The approach from HR is to conduct as much training as possible internally (i. e., training conducted by employees for other employees). For new topics, external experts are involved, especially in "train the trainer" activities. An important part of the current training concept is the onboarding training, which aims to provide basic knowhow and skills to new employees: "*Onboarding is a key step in training for us in finance. There is no onboarding generally for the whole company. That is why we developed our own where we also conduct training on basic skills and knowledge*" (HR Manager, Company 3). Additionally, new "e-learnings" have been introduced: "*Those proved especially helpful when content was to be conveyed. However, for training skills, it's better to use in-person training in groups*" (Manager, Finance Academy, Company 3).

One major challenge of training management accountants is to provide opportunities for individuals to specialize in certain areas while maintaining the standardization happening across the organization: "*We aim at standardizing training further across the whole company.... At least for the basics, we want to have a standard that is taught everywhere*" (Manager, Finance Academy, Company 3). One reason for the (perceived) low support from HR is its focus on other areas of importance: "*The focus of change within the company is on [the] digitization of marketing and developing new marketing and sales concepts. However, I strongly believe that when we introduce new ways of [developing] ... business models, we also have to ensure that supporting functions like management accounting can keep [on] track. Ideally, they would even be involved from the beginning*" (Management Accountant, Company 3).

As mentioned, recruiting efforts and requirements are changing rather slowly at Company 3. Specific changes in skill sets and requirements have not yet been made. However, "*the classic management accountant will ... have to change and think outside the box. He will have to be more open to robotics, toward automation, ... toward process optimization.... [However,] I think that there is not [a] profile or requirement for all but that one has to specify a bit from position to position*" (Team Lead, Management Accounting, Company 3).

5.1.4 Case 4: Mechanical Engineering Company

5.1.4.1 Introduction to Company

Company 4 is a European mechanical engineering company with around 20,000 employees and approximately 5 billion euros in revenues. The multinational company is still family-owned and structured into four divisions, one of which focuses on new, digital business models. Four interviews were conducted in the other three divisions with participants from three major perspectives, which included management accounting, supporting functions (IT), and internal customers (engineering).

5.1.4.2 Overview: Focus on Bottom-up Initiatives Driven by Management Accounting Teams

Company 4 stands apart from the other case companies because digitization is driven much more strongly in the company's positioning toward the market than in the other case companies. It established a new division that focuses on providing digital solutions and business models to its customers. In general, employees at Company 4 do not expect the role and tasks of management accountants to change drastically due to digitization. Management accountants will be responsible for providing support in reporting, planning, and decision-making and view new technologies and digital tools as an opportunity to improve their service to the other functions. With regard to the expected impact on business and profitability, Company 4 differs from the other case companies, as it is a family-owned business, which is not listed on the stock exchange. Hence, there is less pressure to deliver financial results from the digitization projects in the short term. Nevertheless, interviewees underlined the attention of senior managers of the company on projects to drive tangible results. The overall aim, however, is to improve operations with digitization measures and to gain new business in the marketplace. In contrast to the other case companies, cost reductions through digitization is not the primary goal for Company 4.

5.1.4.3 Findings RQ1

Company 4 is undergoing a tremendous transformation of the whole organization, including IT and ERP systems. Consolidation and harmonization are promoted on all levels to prepare for further digitization: "*We're in a change process. We come from a completely heterogeneous world in our divisions and want to become more homogeneous. We currently have four different ERP systems and want to harmonize the data in the long term ... toward one wholistic IT and ERP landscape*" (Management Accountant, Company 4).

At the moment, basic process digitization is highly relevant for management accounting at Company 4. For instance, processes for project monitoring are still conducted partially on paper. Workers hand in the hours they have logged on a project on paper instead of directly booking those hours into an ERP system. Changing processes and making the digital data usable and comparable across the company is a major challenge: "*Only if we manage to digitize the processes around our projects will we be able to fully benefit from digitization. We need to use our own information and data in a structured way. Only then, we'll be able to benefit from new business models that rely on that foundation*" (Management Accountant, Company 4).

The challenge currently is to speed up the change process to be able to spend more time on value-added tasks and reduce manual efforts in reporting and planning. Value-added tasks are those that provide extra information or knowledge to stakeholders, who use the information for their decision-making. The aim is to devote more time to requests and challenges of the business to help internal customers: "*Decision support will be key in the future. We as management accountants need to bring ourselves into a position where it is obvious for everyone that we can help [with] challenging decisions*" (Management Accountant, Company 4).

Management accounting has been driving the implementation of new analytical features to improve decision-making based on data. Furthermore, the visualization of data used to aid decision-making is regarded as an important initiative driven by management accounting.

The implementation of new planning software has been discussed to reduce the manual effort of project calculation and to increase transparency along the project timeline. This is a key challenge that mechanical engineering companies like Company 4 are facing: projects dealing with large machine delivery can often last more than a year from sales to the final delivery. Hence, any improvement in transparency regarding the costs of production and the status of the project is expected to have a substantial impact on performance and profitability. Also, the simulation of changes in external factors such as exchange rate fluctuations would allow for improved preparation and management. Today, the planning is conducted within a relatively static Microsoft Excel tool. However, especially in an engineering company like Company 4, it is necessary to create awareness of the importance of robust reporting and monitoring: "*Improved project planning and management software would help us take the right measures during the time of the project, [such as when] certain assumptions change and impact the cost base of the project*" (Internal Customer, Company 4). For the future, Company 4 aims to handle complex engineering projects better with additional support from project management software that could be applied by management accountants: "*We need to … master complexity better. When calculating scenarios, we need to further make use of tools that, for instance, allow us to change assumptions and drivers of decisions*" (Management Accountant, Company 4).

Company 4 also intends to develop new business models for both itself and for customers who buy machines from them. Hence, the evaluation of new (digital) business models will also be a challenge that management accountants face: "*For instance, the share of software-related business is expected to increase. Management accounting needs to adjust to that development because it's different from the 'plain' machine-building business*" (Manager, IT Project Management Office, Company 4).

In addition to the skills and tools, the general mindset regarding monitoring and controlling projects must be improved to achieve a high acceptance of newly introduced tools: "*Some of our engineers do not really care about monitoring to sufficient detail as long as a project is within budget. However, when a project runs out of the budget and [incurs] losses, it is sometimes too late to react. We need to create transparency with proper project monitoring software and, at the same time, create a sense of urgency in the engineers and project managers*" (Engineer, Company 4).

Another important development, described by IT managers of Company 4, is that digitization leads to faster innovation and a shorter lifespan of existing solutions. Thus, they expect management accountants to face the challenge of adapting their mindset to the more volatile environment: "*In general, … it is always short-lived in the IT world; the changes come in ever shorter cycles, [including] updates and changes in strategy and methods.… Management accounting needs to adapt to it as well by enhancing agility and increasing [their] speed of adaption*" (Manager, IT Project Management Office, Company 4).

5.1.4.4 Findings RQ2

The impact of digitization on the overall organizational structure also affects how management is structured. A new digital solution division has been formed along with a new management accounting team that is responsible for driving the digitization of management accounting in addition to the daily business of supporting the new division. Close collaboration between the new management accounting team and IT is secured, with corporate IT also bundled into the new digital division of Company 4.

Local management accounting units of Company 4 are thus expected to shrink in size due to the higher degree of automation and the ability for each management accountant to cover a larger part of the business, with the help of automated reporting and additional planning and analysis software. Company 4 recently conducted an external benchmark exercise that confirmed a transformation has been taking place. Shared service centers have been introduced to support the further digitization of processes. Traditional accounting tasks are supported by the shared service centers but management accounting has yet to transfer major tasks, although a reporting factory was created, which in the future will be located in the shared service center. Company 4 is centralizing functions that were historically performed within different divisions. The harmonization of the functions and processes is important to further enable digitization and automation: "*To be able to benefit from the digitization and automation in the long run, we need to conduct a lot of groundwork in terms of the standardization and harmonization of processes. Right now, our process landscape is still quite heterogeneous between the divisions*" (Business Process Manager, Company 4). Additionally, the organization is further enhancing its competitiveness through acquisitions in the digital field, such as a digital agency. Especially with regard to speed and resources to build up new competencies, external acquisitions are considered a suitable option for the future.

5.1.4.5 Findings RQ3

With regard to the skills and training needed in the future, the findings from Company 4 do not differ much from the previous cases. The interviewees have ideas on what skills management accountants will need to acquire. However, due to the ongoing reorganization, including forming a new division, no specific concepts for the training and development of management accountants have been developed thus far. As long as there is uncertainty of which and to what degree management accounting functions might be taken over by IT experts or a centralized data management team, the level of IT skills and data literacy to be pursued by management accountants remains unclear. In the long run, IT skills are expected to be indispensable for management accountants, such as a basic understanding of coding. However, there are, to date, no specific adjustments for training and recruiting for specific skills. The same applies to the use of statistical methods and data analytics skills. As is the case with the other companies, employees and teams can push for new training and submit ideas. Nevertheless, an overall training concept preparing employees for the challenges of digitization has not been introduced yet.

5.1.5 Case 5: Automotive Supplier

5.1.5.1 Introduction to Company

Company 5 is a tier-1 publicly listed automotive supplier with more than 300,000 employees and over 50 billion euros in revenues. The corporate headquarters and the headquarters of all four business divisions are located in Central Europe. In total, three interviews were conducted with employees and managers from one of the business divisions, covering the perspective of a manager in management accounting, a supporting function (HR), and an internal customer of the management accounting function (R&D).

5.1.5.2 Overview

At Company 5, changes triggered from bottom-up and top-down have impacted the digitization of the management accounting function. On the one hand, there are measures and projects to increase efficiency that are initiated and closely monitored by top management. On the other hand, the interviewees described initiatives that are clearly driven by the management accountants: "*I am a big supporter of my team members who drive new initiatives and bring up ideas to use data. However, we always try to analyze only data for specific questions we try to answer. We don't want to analyze random data into the blue just for the purpose of doing 'big data'. What we are trying to do is to use new technologies and skills but still … be efficient in the way we work*" (Manager, Controlling, Company 5). In sum, ideas for change and digitization projects that affect management accounting have been driven by various stakeholders in diverse hierarchical levels. However, Company 5's top management has not set efficiency improvement goals for management accounting (e.g., in terms of the number of employees in the management accounting function).

Interviewees also pointed out that Company 5 aims to establish experts for new analytical tasks on different hierarchy levels and teams, rather than forming new teams that solely focus on big data analytics.

5.1.5.3 Findings RQ1

As mentioned earlier, in Company 5, changes that impact the tasks and tools in management accounting were triggered from bottom-up and top-down: "*In our company, there are initiatives that are driven by single employees or teams that have an idea, [such as] introducing a new planning tool for the manufacturing function. However, there are also centrally planned initiatives that are driven from top management across the whole division, [such as reducing] costs by standardizing the ERP systems further, which obviously has a large impact on management accounting*" (Head of Manufacturing Controlling, Company 5). The bottom-up-driven changes have included the introduction of more sophisticated (big data) analytics tools and the inclusion of larger sets of data, as well as new kinds of data. One of the major challenges that the management accountants have faced and tackled with the help of the IT function has been the existence of various data pools across different functions, which were not coherently organized and structured. Management accounting aims to make the data usable and eventually connect the data pools. With the broader picture in mind, management accounting can now have a clear understanding of what sort of data analysis is available across different functions and thus avoid depleting resources on tasks that might not be beneficial or acquiring resources that already exist.

The top-down-driven digitization in Company 5 focuses especially on standardization within and between the different divisions of the large conglomerate. One of the company's long-term projects is the standardization of ERP solutions used by management accountants (and all other functions). The objective is to reduce maintenance and programming costs because the various locations, divisions, and functions have been using customized solutions from different providers. In addition, the project aims to enable different teams to share knowledge, data, and new solutions they have developed, such as dashboards. The major motivation, however, is to allow the use of data across different functions and geographies for more holistic decision-making. Historically, the management accounting function is closely structured along the functions of the company—there is a team that supports manufacturing and another team that focuses on the support of R&D by providing planning, reporting, and decision support. With the help of digitization, Company 5 aims to provide better support to each function by improving the collaboration and data sharing between the management accounting teams of the various functions.

5.1.5.4 Findings RQ2

Organizationally, Company 5 currently has shared service centers in use; however, there are no specific tasks outsourced for management accounting into shared service centers yet. However, this might be a future option. The use of shared service centers in management accounting also depends on the further development of the divisions of Company 5. Currently, the divisions operate independently and, hence, every division uses shared service centers in their own way. However, if there is further centralization in the future, shared service centers might also be used to a higher degree in management accounting.

Company 5 aims to introduce and develop data analytics experts at different levels of management accounting but there are no plans to develop new teams or units of analytics. However, one can conclude that with regard to management accounting and its organizational setup, no radical changes have been implemented.

One reason for that is the unclear path of the company going forward regarding the structure—rumors range from further separation to an IPO of one of the four divisions.

5.1.5.5 Findings RQ3

At Company 5, discussions are ongoing on the skills and training needed to prepare management accountants for the future. First ideas are being detailed and HR is planning to derive a concept on skill profiles and new training, but specific adjustments have not yet been applied. The necessity to do so is recognized by the team leads in management accounting and also by the HR business partner responsible for the management accounting employees.

With regard to the skills needed in the future, it stood out that some IT skills are expected to be needed by management accountants, such as the ability to deal with new software and to understand basic coding structures. Because no decision has been made on covering certain data analytics skills, no detailed plan on to what extent each management accountant needs to be able to handle, for example, coding languages like Python could be derived. If a data analytics team is established within management accounting, not all management accountants would have to possess detailed skills. However, without a central analytics unit within management accounting, management accountants themselves would have to be able to apply a higher level of data analytics skills.

From the perspective of the internal client, it would be very helpful to have management accountants at hand who are able to analyze large datasets and support decision-making. However, the gap between what management accountants are currently able to do at Company 5 and the level of suggested support is described as rather large: "*A high amount and depth of training would be necessary to establish a management accounting function on a companywide level that is able to support decision-making with in-depth analytic skills and, at the same time, a good understanding of the business itself. Right now, I only can imagine this to be feasible in the far future. As of now, management accountants are still occupied very much with creating reports and gathering data manually rather than adding value in terms of analytical work and decision support*" (Head of R&D of One Division, Company 5).

The complexity of the products and processes of Company 5 makes the tasks for management accountants even more challenging because, ideally, a management accountant would also have a background or at least a good understanding of the products and production processes to be able to further grow into an advisory role: "*In the long run, we should aim [to develop] our management accountants toward skill profiles that allow them to advise management on important decisions. However, to do so, it is not just necessary to grow them in terms of IT skills and statistics due to large amounts ... and new kinds of data—it is also necessary for them to gain a better understanding of the product ... to be able to apply judgment. As of now, I think we are ... too far away from the business ... to give valuable advice on business decisions, which is not just based on financials*" (Management Accountant, Company 5). However, the required skills and their development is closely related to the (expected) changes in tasks that are not yet fully implemented. Hence, the next milestone is to develop concepts for preparing the management accountants for the new tasks.

5.2 Summary: Impact of Digitization on Tasks and Tools on Management Accounting Function in Manufacturing Organizations

According to the case study results, management accountants and related functions predict diverse changes with respect to the tasks and tools of management accounting as a result of digitization. Supporting the decision-making of the management team is expected to remain the main objective of management accounting functions; it is the means by which to reach the goals resulting from digitization.

In fact, the daily work and tasks of management accounting have already been changing, and more changes are expected. New management accounting tasks, such as the analysis of new kinds of data, have emerged and a shift in focus from reporting and planning to decision support is taking place. Data management and data visualization are gaining importance (as indicated, for instance, by Company 2). In the past, more time and resources were spent on reporting and planning because management accountants manually generated reports and prepared planning and budgeting processes. Under digitization, these tasks are being further automated, partly with the help of shared service centers. Benefiting from the division of labor and automation, larger volumes of data can be processed and analyzed more efficiently. Hence, faster and better-informed decision support is possible for the management accounting functions.

Additionally, in the interviews, the management accountants stressed that the transformation of the company and the function itself brings with it additional tasks. For instance, the setup of a data warehouse involves close cooperation between management accounting and the IT function. For management accounting, it is crucial to be involved in these kinds of projects to be able to work with and shape the new infrastructure and, hence, be able to add value in the future. The same applies when ERP systems are consolidated (as shown, for instance, in Company 4). IT specialists might have a different perspective when making decisions regarding technology changes. Thus, it is important for management accounting to position itself to drive the transformational projects that are related to their function, so they are as close to the desired setup as possible to allow for smooth cooperation and, most importantly, to provide the maximum benefits. These transformational tasks are a pre-requisite for the future value-add of management accounting and the position (or even the existence) of management accounting. Management accounting needs to provide extra information and knowledge to the organization and stakeholders that they would otherwise not have.

In addition to new tasks, traditional accounting tasks are changing in the way they are executed. The amount of resources and time needed for tasks is also changing. When it comes to reporting, the preparation of inputs for reports is automated and reports can be automatically downloaded from the ERP systems. As described for Company 4, reporting factories are introduced and established mainly in shared service centers. The employees in the shared service centers conduct "sanity" checks on data that are used in reports and prepare new formats. The repetitive tasks of compiling reports are reduced to a low level. Instead, local management accounting teams focus on commenting and data interpretation in reports based on their knowledge of the business and the (financial) data. With regard to reporting, the formats of reports and the process of producing and sharing reports have been impacted by new technologies. Only a few reports are sent via email to the audience group. The focus is on sharing reports on platforms and on sharing data via dashboards. This trend toward self-service reporting (as shown, for instance, in Company 3) is strengthened by the increase in the use of smartphones and tablets. Managers and other users of reporting data view the information via a smartphone app or desktop program rather than receiving files via email.

Digitalization is also impacting management accounting in terms of planning and budgeting. New software has been introduced to support planning processes, such as for visualization and also to provide further agility and flexibility in planning scenarios (e.g. in Company 4). When planning various scenarios, new software solutions provide the opportunity to include forecasts calculated by algorithms based on historical data. Additionally, they make the planning process more collaborative rather than merely sharing Excel files in which managers must manually fill in their assumptions. With digitization, assumptions are no longer arbitrarily made by managers—they are based on historical data whereby forecasts are produced. The process is further objectified by backing up and checking assumptions based on historical data and forecasts produced by algorithms. This is the major difference from the past, when managers often based budgets and plans on their experience and intuition rather than on specific data.

As described previously, decision support is expected to become the main task of management accountants, who will foster and maintain a closer working relationship with decision-makers. Time spent on tasks will shift: "*Whereas nowadays, still quite a lot of resources are needed for reporting, in the future, the management accountant will focus on more value-creating tasks in giving advice to decision-makers. A report that took me several hours in the past can be created automatically out of the ERP system*" (Management Accountant, Company 3).

Furthermore, the amount of automation in the execution of tasks is increasing. This is especially relevant for reporting tasks, as previously described. Also, the automation of single steps in planning (e.g., scenarios or just single drivers of performance, such as demand) is expected. In addition, new technologies like RPA (as short to mid-term solutions if various tools need to be "connected") allow the management accountant to focus on interpreting data rather than on creating reports or documents manually. Repetitive processes are expected to be automated as much as possible because it is faster, cheaper, and less likely to result in mistakes compared to work done manually by a management accountant: "*[A]utomation in the execution of tasks will increase further. Tasks that are today conducted by colleagues in management accounting, [such as] creating reports, is already and will be further executed automatically*" (IT Manager, Company 2).

As mentioned earlier, new software will be used to gain further insights from data that have not been previously included in decision-making. New solutions are being introduced for single tasks (e.g., planning), certain types of data, and whole new systems (eg., consolidated ERP system). The use of artificial intelligence and machine learning is also expected to gain importance. For management accountants, these technologies are especially interesting because they reveal relationships that humans do not expect or look for; this is possible because large amounts of data and datasets can be included in the search for correlations. With the increasing numbers of new tools and innovations arises mounting complexity that needs to be addressed by management accountants: "*The tasks of the management accountant will not just be to understand and analyze complex issues but also to visualize and communicate the issues to managers that are not involved closely*" (Management Accountant, Company 5). When handling complexity, problem-solving skills will be crucial: "*Because repetitive tasks will be further automated, the management accountant will often handle tasks that he has not faced before. Hence, problem-solving in a business context based on data will be key*" (Commercial Director, Company 2).

5.3 Summary: Impact of Digitization on Organizational Structure of Management Accounting Function in Manufacturing Organizations

RQ2 investigated the impact of digitization on the organizational and geographical structure of management accounting functions in manufacturing organizations. The outlook is that management accounting will still follow the organizational setup of the line functions that management accountants support. Overall, there should not be a fundamental shift of the management accounting structure.

Shared service centers are an important aspect of organizational structure and play a critical role in the management accounting functions of manufacturing companies. They have been in use for years by large corporations. The size and the individual situation of the company usually influence the extent to which tasks are transferred to shared service centers: "*For us, shared service centers have recently played a more ... important role. We try to further shift tasks to SSCs and to standardize processes. This is still an ongoing process. Obviously, within the shared service centers, we try to further automate tasks ... to reduce overhead in the centers*" (Expert, Shared Service Center [not from one of the case companies]). For Company 1, cost reduction is at the top of the agenda in preparation for a large acquisition. Thus, a significant number of tasks are being transferred to shared service centers, which is essential to reach cost-reduction targets. In contrast, Company 4 makes very limited use of shared service centers. The strategic focus of the corporation is on benefiting from new growth markets rather than reducing costs. When comparing these two cases, one has to keep in mind the difference in company size. With regard to digitization, the use of shared service centers is an accelerator of standardization and the automation of tasks. Tasks such as the preparation of a recurring report are standardized, bundled, and automated in shared service centers, where the potential for further automation is analyzed. Certain duties such as bookkeeping and classic accounting tasks have a higher potential to be automated. Reporting and other repetitive analyses are automated as much as possible in shared service centers.

To achieve the ever-stricter cost-reduction targets, companies could also consider outsourcing tasks, going one step further than bundling them in shared service centers. The case companies are extremely cautious in considering this step for management accounting tasks due to data security reasons, as well as the importance of the decisions that are supported by management accounting. Hence, while trying to optimize cost savings, the aim is still to keep the important processes in-house.

In addition to shared service centers, new organizational units and teams are formed to handle data analytics within management accounting. Interestingly, data analytics units have been established in several functions of the case study organizations. Instead of establishing a central data analytics team that serves, for example, marketing, finance, or management accounting, the companies opt to establish smaller data specialist units within the functions. They argue that a close relation to and understanding of the function itself is necessary to conduct data analytics efficiently. However, it also becomes obvious that within all the case companies, the resources of data specialists are scarce. Hence, one could question the approach of multiplying the resource across the functions and argue for further centralization of data analytics experts.

With regard to the size of the management accounting functions and teams, the majority of the interviewees expect an overall decrease in the number of management accountants. Automation and support of tools allow management accountants to conduct, for instance, reporting, planning, and budgeting much faster than in the past. Additionally, a shift is expected from local management accounting teams (e.g., for a single location or region) toward centralized teams. Local management accounting teams are expected to rely further on support from specialists in centralized teams for data analytics or from shared service centers. Hence, the number of employees needed for analyses and repetitive tasks like creating data files and reports is expected to decrease. The local management accounting teams are expected to focus further on the business partnering role while benefiting from the support of centralized teams.

The second RQ2 question deals with the drivers and barriers of management accounting digitization in manufacturing companies. Drivers and barriers described by interviewees embraced a wide range, from the personal motivation of employees and decision-makers to the organizational structure and the overall market strategy.

The need to digitize the management accounting function is mainly driven by strategic or operational needs to meet market requirements. For example, for a company in a cost-reduction phase, the ability to reduce cost with the digitization of management accounting (and other functions) is a major driver of conducting digitization measures. Furthermore, the digitization of all functions, including management accounting, is used to drive growth and to improve operations. Overall, from the perspective of the firm, managers and management accountants aim to contribute to the goals of the firm to improve decision-making with the help of digitalized management accounting. This can entail supporting decision-making at lower costs (e.g., with fewer employees), as well as using new technology to make better decisions (e.g., to analyze data using artificial intelligence). These measures are indirectly driven by fierce competition in the industry, which forces companies to improve.

Another driver of digitalization is top management attention. As with other initiatives, often the top-down-driven approach of change raises attention quickly: "*[I]t is still important to have top management commitment for the initiative. Because our top management started the project and assigned cost-saving targets to each function and team, everyone knows it and sets it as high priority*" (Management Accountant, Company 5). Corporate culture also plays a role, especially when it comes to bottom-up-driven measures. Innovative and R&D-driven organizations tend to allow employees (also in management accounting) to be more creative in testing new solutions in terms of tools or when problems arise. Another factor driving the digitalization of management accounting is learning from the digitalization of other functions. However, interviewees pointed out that management accounting is not viewed as the frontrunner of digitalization in most companies.

On the other hand, the interviewees described organizational and personal barriers for the digitalization of management accounting. Organizational barriers, such as the complexity of introducing a new IT tool and the heterogeneity of tools and systems across regions, functions, and business units, inhibit management accounting from making changes. Furthermore, the limitation of resources is a significant barrier against digitization for some companies. As with other change initiatives, digitalization often requires an upfront investment that can be difficult to justify with hard facts. Not every introduction of a new tool can be argued for with quantitative results on revenues or the costs of a company but could potentially improve decision-making and, hence, the market position in the long run. With regard to companywide change, the heterogeneity of business models, structures, and markets among business units can be a barrier because it incurs complexity in terms of organizational units as well as IT systems that are in place. If business units or divisions are formed and managed independently, it makes it difficult to standardize tasks and centralize specialist functions. Also, in these cases, divisions are often compared in terms of results and compete rather than cooperate, which inhibits introducing digitization in the same direction and manner. The corporate culture also adds to this argument. As previously mentioned, a corporate culture open to innovation can be expected to welcome change, whereas a closed, conservative culture can be a barrier for change.

In addition to the structure and nature of the business, the agenda, intentions, and ability of individuals in supporting digitalization could act as a barrier. Individuals could have their personal benefits in mind rather than organizational benefits when driving or inhibiting change in a company. A management accountant could, for instance, refrain from driving the automation of tasks because he is afraid of losing his job when a new tool is able to generate a report in a few seconds that the employee previously required a few hours' time to create. This motivation and agenda of single employees are closely related to the ability to adapt to new developments. Hence, the (felt) inability to handle new solutions and to develop oneself further can also be a barrier to change.

5.4 Summary: Impact of Digitization on Skills and Training of Management Accounting Function in Manufacturing Organizations

As described in detail for the five cases, companies recognize a necessary change in the skill set of the management accountants. Managers, HR employees, and management accountants expect a slight change in the background of management accountants and an extensive need for training in order to remain important to the company and to allow them to cope with new technologies and tasks.

Although the companies differ in terms of new skill sets required from management accountants, a general mastering of standard management accounting tools and instruments (as taught in college), as well as basic knowledge in accounting, finance, and other adjacent business administration topics is expected to still be crucial. The same applies to communication and persuasion skills and the ability to ask critical questions. Companies that are introducing a new business partnering role, for instance, emphasized a greater focus on communication skills. This kind of role demands management accountants to be closer to management and decision-makers; therefore, the communication of a proposed decision will gain further importance.

When it comes to IT knowledge, however, the need for different backgrounds depends on the tasks and structure of management accounting, as well as IT, in the company. However, the majority of management accountants agree that general data and IT literacy is important for every management accountant: "*[I]t is key that a management accountant brings some data literacy to the table. However, not every management accounting needs to be able to develop algorithms. General understanding and interest in data is a must-have*" (Management Accountant, Company 3).

Even if they do not conduct complex analyses, management accountants are expected to have a general understanding of and ability to interpret results. Additionally, companies are creating specialist roles to bolster their data analytics capabilities. For those specialists, deeper knowledge of data mining methodologies will be required compared to management accountants.

Although the interviewees from the five case companies described their expectations regarding the skills that might be needed in the future, none of them were able to illustrate a detailed concept of the desired skill set(s) and the ways to develop employees toward those skill sets. Nevertheless, the case companies provided first ideas on how to adapt the training, education, and recruiting of the management accountant of the future.

According to one HR manager, agility will be key in the future, including in corporate learning. Training and seminars will have to be adapted more often to the rapidly changing reality than in the past. This does not just apply to management accounting but to many other functions.

Another important topic is life-long learning. Employees will have to adjust more often to keep up with new requirements during their careers. Careers and the outlook of management accountants will differ depending on the time they have spent in various functions, positions, and probably even companies. In other words, management accountants will not carry the same profile across the board; however, while technology is gaining momentum, management accountants need to catch up and keep pace.

The training curriculum will need to consist of a more extensive mix of methods. Training on the job, specialist training using external resources, and e-learnings are just a few sources used to educate and transfer knowledge to employees. External and cross-functional training is expected to be vital to keep up with technological developments: "*In terms of training and education, I think we still need a mix of methods because different people learn differently and different contents are taught better in different ways. When it comes to content, I really think we should update and improve our training … to keep up with the challenges and developments we face in management accounting but also in other functions*" (HR Business Partner, Company 5).

With regard to the desired profiles of new graduate employees, the opinions differ slightly among the case companies because it depends on the role within management accounting that needs to be filled. However, the interviewees expect the majority of graduate employees still to have a business and finance degree. If applicable, a stronger focus on IT and the ability to deal with larger amounts of data and statistics will be required. The bottom line of the discussions was, in most cases, that the management accountant needs to bridge the understanding of the business and the financials, with the ability to conduct technology-driven analyses to prepare for decisions. Whereas in the past, analytical tasks and tool familiarity was mostly learned on the job, in the future, candidates will be expected to have a greater IT focus and experience with various IT tools, as well as higher data literacy. For specialist roles such as data scientists, focused backgrounds in their fields (e.g., math and statistics) are expected. Because the advisory part of the management accountant job is anticipated to gain importance, better communication skills are expected to be needed in the future, as previously mentioned: "*Communication skills are important to be able to act as [a] business partner. The management accountant needs to be able to communicate complex issues to managers. This will become even more important, as the management accountant will spend more of his time [providing] consulting [for] management or a line function*" (Management Accountant, Company 3).

One of the interesting and revealing outcomes of the interviews was the difference in expectations and opinions between the HR function and management accounting on HR's role in supporting digitization. Management accounting interviewees currently describe it as a pull rather than push relationship; in other words, management accountants must actively seek support from HR, which is very limited and passive: "*To be honest, I have never waited or relied on HR for training. When I have something I'm interested in, I will approach my boss and he will get the approval from HR for me to attend the training. However, I know that most colleagues are not as proactive. Therefore, it might be helpful to have a better training guideline and advice ... to develop the teams further*" (Management Accountant, Company 3). Conceptual support from HR on the development of employees is expected for the future because this is relevant for all functions, not just management accounting. HR managers agree on the need for further support; however, resources and the focus have traditionally been on supporting rather than changing the functions of a company. Hence, the HR function itself also must adapt to fulfill the needs of the other functions, which requires resources and knowledge that, in many cases, must be built up. It is challenging for HR to transform from a predominantly administrative role toward a visionary one. Also, the unclear vision on what management accounting will have to provide in the future makes the task difficult for HR: "*[I]t is difficult to trigger change, as we do not have a clear view on how management accountants' profiles should look like in the future. We are in discussion with the leadership team, but even they are having a hard time [coming] up with a vision ... for us to derive training concepts*" (HR Business Partner, Company 1).

5.5 Grounded Model: Two Archetypes of Digitization in Management Accounting

In this section, the empirical findings are presented for the five case companies. The patterns that emerged from the analysis of the qualitative information are described and discussed. Two distinct archetypes of change emerged with respect to the digitization of the management accounting function. These archetypes were derived from the findings for RQ1 and RQ2 for the five cases. The first archetype, which was called "streamlining" by the author, applies only to Company 1, which drives the digitization of management accounting top-down and focuses on cost reduction. The second archetype applies to three of the five case companies and refers to an approach that focuses on revenue growth with the support of management accounting digitization. Only Company 5 does not apply clearly one of the two approaches but rather a mixture of both. An overview of the cases and their archetype is shown in Fig. 5.1.

	Case 1	Case 2	Case 3	Case 4	Case 5
Revenues [bn EUR]	20–50	1-10	1-10	1-10	20–50
Employees ['000]	> 100	> 10-20	>10-20	>10-20	>100
Industry	Pharma & Chemicals	Consumer Goods	Consumer Goods	Mechanical Engineering	Automotive supplier
Archetype	Streamlining	Enabling	Enabling	Enabling	Mix
Interviews [#]	4	3	7	4	3

Fig. 5.1 Summary of cases (Lachmann & Holtkemper, 2021)

5.5.1 Streamlining: Efficiency Focused

The first archetype of change focuses on rationalizing and streamlining the existing management accounting function. The main objective of this archetype is to increase the efficiency and cost-effectiveness of management accounting; in other words, to conduct the same analyses and tasks with fewer resources and in less time. The approach is driven primarily from top-down—cost-saving targets are determined by senior management and measures, including the digitization and automation of tasks and processes, are implemented as a means to achieve these targets. The overall cost-saving target for the company is broken down into specific targets for the different functions and teams. During the implementation, the achievement of the targets is monitored closely to ensure that the overall target of standardizing and reducing costs is reached. The goal of these measures and initiatives is to ensure standardization and to ease the automation of processes and tasks (e.g., RPA in the accounting function and dashboard solutions based on standardized data). Also, the planning process tends to become leaner because the manual work of the management accounting function is minimized (e.g., assembling data and filling out forms).

In this archetype of digital change, the focus of local management accounting teams shifts toward an advisory role to management and other tasks are passed to shared service centers, in which tasks are further standardized and automated where applicable. The aim is to reduce the number of repetitive tasks that have traditionally been carried out by management accounting employees to complete tasks more quickly, at a lower cost, and with fewer mistakes with the help of digitization and the automation of processes. The number of employees needed in local management accounting teams is therefore expected to decrease because resources are centralized in shared service centers. One can link the characteristics of companies with an efficiency focus (such as Company 1) to the theories described in the organizational perspective (as described in Chapter 3). The aim of the company is to maximize efficiency, which is also what has been detailed under the theoretical considerations regarding economies of scale (Henderson, 1968).

5.5.2 Enabling: Value-Added Focused

The second archetype focuses primarily on the advanced value-add improvement of the management accounting function. This type of company specifically aims to improve its analytics capabilities in order to improve decision made my management. Measures and projects include substantial investments in new software tools and infrastructure (e.g., ERP systems), use of additional data sources that have previously not been commonly considered in the management accounting context (eg., machine data to rationalize further cost forecasts for investment decisions in machinery and maintenance), and the use of new technologies, such as artificial intelligence. More specifically, innovation and new features are implemented to improve processes and tasks. For example, in the planning process, new software is used (e.g., scenario planning tools) to increase flexibility in planning and transparency on how the adjustment of assumptions affects the outcome. Accordingly, new features are introduced into the reporting capabilities of companies, such as dashboard solutions that provide real-time data on portable devices like mobile phones and tablets. Instead of sending in requests for each individual report needed, which would then be compiled in the appropriate department, a self-service dashboard enables a sales representative to quickly tailor and review relevant data at any chosen time, such as prior to a client meeting. These innovations and developments consequently improve the day-to-day decision-making processes across the organization with higher efficiency because additional and more up-to-date data is incorporated, making decisions more well-informed. The overall aim of the companies is to create transparency and encourage more objective decision-making, eliminating decisions based on intuition. Management accounting aims to add value to their organizations by providing additional information and knowledge for decision-making.

Furthermore, heightened technological complexity and the need for data analytics skills affect the organizational structure of the management accounting function. To master the increasingly complex technological changes and shift in focus toward a data-driven advisory role, experts must be recruited for or trained within management accounting teams. Large corporations may form entirely new specialist teams focusing on data analytics to provide support for local management accounting teams. Because these capabilities cannot be offered in every local entity, local management accounting teams can request support, for instance, when they are unable to analyze an unstructured dataset. The specialist team supports and shares new solutions across the whole management accounting organization while continuously developing new analytical features and integrating these into standardized processes to benefit local management accounting teams with their expertise.

Overall, the archetype is driven from bottom-up by employees who come up with new ideas and innovations. The aim is to improve the decision-making process and to simplify complex tasks by utilizing tools and technologies. The extent to which the management accounting teams drive new solutions depends on the freedom and time given to innovate in addition to their daily work. Another important factor that drives innovation is the close collaboration between the internal customer (e.g., user of the reports) and the management accountants. Management accountants, who align closely with customer needs, tend to be innovation-driven and often try to provide new solutions to their internal customers. The support of the IT functions and the degree to which the management accounting team is able to develop their own IT capabilities are also crucial elements to realize changes.

With regard to the theories introduced in Chapter 3, the characteristics of the value-added focused archetype link to the individual perspective, i.e. to Social Exchange theory and also to the (reduction of) heuristics and biases in decision processes. The intended improvement of fact-based decision-making processes can lead to reduction of biases and heuristics since decisions are made rather objective based on facts and data. However, the introduction of self-service reporting tools could also lead to an increase in managers falling victim to biases since they might be tempted to use the self-service tool to justify gut-based decision without having a management accountant as counterpart. This way of reasoning also connects to the Social Exchange Theory because employees might trigger and focus on specific changes which allow them to maximize their own benefit.

5.6 Change of Positioning and Trends with Regard to the Discovered Archetypes

Based on the interviews, the case companies were categorized into the two archetypes described, as shown in Fig. 5.2. Because change is an ever-evolving process, the positioning of the case companies is not fixed. There are tendencies of the companies to move toward the middle of the grid, adopting a balanced approach, or to focus on one extreme after concentrating on the other for a period of time. After a trial period of forming a new big data team, Company 2 realized that their hopes would not materialize. Hence, the management team decided to halt investments and instead focus on building a leaner structure in which standard tasks can be conducted with the least resources possible. Their decision is to move toward an approach of digitization that aims no longer to increase value-add but to reduce costs instead. In the matrix, the case companies do not position themselves in the top-right or bottom-left quadrant.

For those case companies in the top-right quadrant in Fig. 5.2, the change toward standardization, automation, and, subsequently, the need for fewer resources is not driven bottom-up by the employees in the management accounting function. Naturally, employees do not possess the motivation to save costs by reducing the number of resources in management accounting because they will not benefit from this action. Employees will try to avoid these measures because they might face putting their own team or team members at risk.

In the companies shown in the bottom-left quadrant in Fig. 5.2, the implementation of new tools and software to improve analytics and the focus on making the management accountants' jobs easier is mostly driven from bottom-up, not top-down. Senior management does not have to be as close to the tasks to drive change. Additionally, the change progress is on a request-budget basis; in other words, employees and teams request additional funds when they want to launch an initiative for a new tool. Digitization innovations in terms of new tools (with the exception of general investments in ERP systems) are driven based on demand rather than on a digital agenda for management accounting.

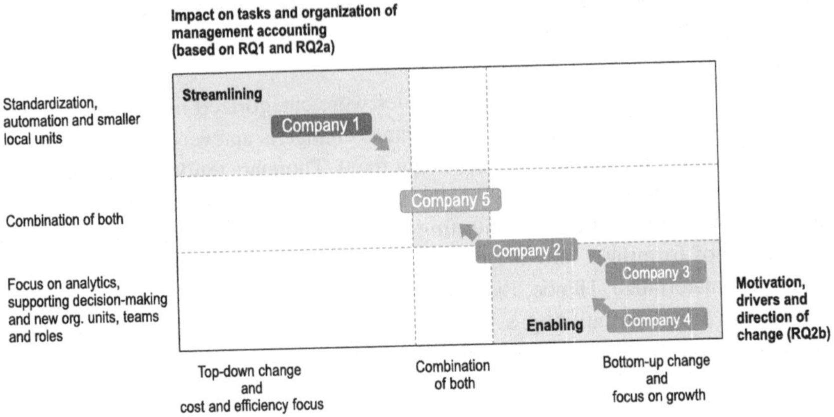

Fig. 5.2 Archetypes (Lachmann & Holtkemper, 2021)

5.7 Relation of Strategy to the Digitization of Management Accounting (RQ4)

For each of the case companies, the relation of the approach of digitization in management accounting with the overall strategy was analyzed. The discussion and analysis were structured into three stages. First, the general strategic direction stated in recent annual reports and company presentations was reviewed. Next, the overall approach of the company toward digitization was discussed with the interviewees. Finally, specific strategic measures and projects to reduce costs and increase efficiency were examined. The analysis of the strategy was then set into relation to the patterns analyzed regarding the digitization of management accounting.

For instance, for Company 1 (with a top-down-driven change approach for management accounting), cost reduction is a major element within the overall company strategy. Management accounting is regarded as a cost position rather than an analytical unit for support in decision-making (which in turn could also lead to cost reductions).

Company 5, which deploys a mixed approach, describes its strategy using terms like "sustainable growth" and "balanced portfolio." Management accounting measures are in line with the strategy of balancing growth and optimizing the existing business. In contrast to other case companies, there is no focus on either only top-down (cost-focused) measures or initiatives driven bottom-up.

Bottom-up-driven approaches are applied in companies that aim to grow via new digital opportunities. However, in cases in which growth measures do not succeed, a shift in strategy toward cost reduction is applied (as shown in Company 3). Overall, the results of the analysis indicate that management accounting is treated in the same way in terms of digitization as other units within the companies.

To relate the digitization efforts in the management accounting function back to the overall business strategy, the strategy was analyzed based on the interviews and additional documents provided by the case companies in their investor portals and presentations. The analysis was based on the Porter (1985) framework discussed in the theory section regarding cost and differentiation strategies. Additionally, strategic digitization efforts of the whole company were a focus.

5.7.1 Case 1: Pharma and Chemicals Conglomerate

Company 1's corporate publications (i.e., annual reports and investor presentations) state the key strategic pillars of the firm, including "innovation, customer focus, quality, process excellence, and portfolio management." Of these strategic pillars, process excellence and portfolio management were heavily discussed and described as important by the interviewees. The pillars of innovation, customer focus, and quality were not focused on by the interviewees. Hence, one could argue that the internal direction of Company 1 within the management accounting context differs to some extent from the strategic direction published for external stakeholders. Process excellence was a key theme in the context of cost reduction and the optimization of processes with the help of digitization and automation. Referring to Porter (1985), one could argue that there is no focus on cost leadership or differentiation. Alternatively, one could contend that the cost focus, which became apparent during the interviews, is only temporarily applied to focus resources and enable innovation in the future. Based on further analysis of press releases and the interviews, portfolio optimization is a key focus that is conducted mainly through the acquisition of a larger major competitor. In preparation for the integration of the acquired company, the focus is on improving the current cost structure and processes to merge the acquired company into an optimized company with lean structures. In this context, management accounting was analyzed for its cost-optimization potential. The management accounting function had to achieve cost-reduction targets, as did all the other functions. Process optimization and the adaption of structures play an important role. With regard to cost measures, one division recently announced on Company 1's website that it will undergo "further optimization of cost structures." The digitization efforts of Company 1 focus on gaining a competitive advantage in the markets. New digital offerings (e.g., digital farming and agriculture) have been developed in-house and were a major argument for the acquisition of the other company. By acquiring the competitor, Company 1's goal is to improve its positioning in digital offerings because this is where the competitor has a stronger market position.

However, one can conclude from the analysis of strategic publications and the interviews that the focus of the whole company now is to reduce costs and to optimize structures. This strategic direction is applied to management accounting, as well as other functions. Digitization for Company 1 is a means to achieve these ambitious cost-reduction targets.

5.7.2 Case 2: Beverage Manufacturer

Company 2's overall strategy described in their publications focuses on finding new areas of growth. Because Company 2 is the leader in a market segment that is no longer growing, it is in search of additional market segments with growth potential and in taking growth measures in the traditional markets to increase market share. In addition to organic growth measures such as pricing and the use of new sales channels, the acquisition of other companies and brands in related markets play an important role. For instance, the company recently bought a coffee chain to grow in the relevant segment.

During the course of this study, efficiency measures in Europe were announced by Company 2. These measures included plant closures and job cuts in Germany, the outsourcing of finance and accounting jobs, and the application of a zero-based work approach. As previous ambitious growth targets could not be reached, management adjusted structures and reduced costs to mitigate the loss of profitability. The zero-based work approach focuses on the value-add of every process and function and, thus, its necessity for the business. Non-value-added processes that are not resulting in important additional information or knowledge are to be eliminated or reduced.

This adaption of the growth strategy to an increasing cost focus could also be observed in the digitization efforts of the management accounting function. A newly established big data team was dismantled shortly after it had been established, as it had failed to convince management of its value and ability to provide measures for growth.

When communicating strategic directions, the management of Company 2 describes digitizing the company as one of the main strategic pillars. Digitization efforts toward consumers are important, as is internal digitization. The company's website explicitly states that the aim is to "put actionable data to work inside our enterprise, liberate resources through the use of technology and share data-based learnings across teams and functions."

5.7.3 Case 3: Consumer Goods Company

Company 3's recent strategic program has been focusing on strengthening brands and driving innovation in emerging markets. Strategy presentations and publications indicate a focus on generating further growth, with emerging markets at the core of its strategy.

Company 3 aims to utilize digitization for approaching customers and markets. A stronger digital presence toward customers is one of the strategic targets set by the management. Internally, the focus on digitization measures is, according to public statements, on e-learning and the development of employees.

Overall, strategic announcements in annual reports and investor presentations suggest that Company 3 aims to utilize digitization to generate profitable growth rather than to reduce costs. Management accounting is considered vital in supporting the daily business with new tools and data for implementing the growth strategy.

5.7.4 Case 4: Mechanical Engineering Company

Digitization plays an important role in Company 4's strategic focus. The importance has also been signaled to the market by establishing a new division focusing on digital solutions for customers. Overall, the short-term focus is on growth initiatives after a reorganization with the addition of the new division.

Company 4 proactively communicates that the digital transformation is ongoing in the market but also in the company itself. The ambitious aim of the company is to further develop toward being a digital leader in the market. To realize the goal, it has defined a digital agenda that not only includes the formation of the new division but also the development of new products (e.g., an online marketplace) and the further growth of digital competencies organically as well as through acquisitions of digital companies (e.g., a digital agency).

With regard to efficiency and cost-reduction measures, further optimization of processes and structures have been mentioned in the company's publications. However, the focus clearly is on growth in the traditional and new businesses.

Company 4 is mainly driving digitization by adjusting its structures internally, which will provide new market solutions and products. Management accounting is involved in the reorganization and the strategic focus on digitization. It is set to be developed further to support growth in times of digitization. It is worth noting that cost reduction is not in focus for the management accounting function. Overall, the focus of the company and the way digitization is incorporated into management accounting are going in the same direction for the foreseeable future.

5.7.5 Case 5: Automotive Supplier

The overall strategic direction of Company 5 has been in seven areas of action, including, for instance, sustainability as an overarching target and a balanced portfolio strategy. The company is facing shifts in the market environment. As a major automotive supplier, the digitization and electrification of the mobility sector have played an important role in Company 5's strategy. Hence, one focus of the corporate strategy is on developing new technological solutions for the mobility sector, especially the automotive segment. As of today, a large proportion of sales are related to digital technologies in the automotive segment, which shows that the transformation is ongoing and that Company 5 has been, thus far, successful at adapting to the changing market conditions.

With regard to the impact of digitization on the internal functions, structures, and processes, the focus is on HR and the impact of digitization and automation on employees in general, according to its public communications. The emphasis, however, is on blue-collar workers rather than on supporting functions such as management accounting. The company has communicated that measures have been put in place to prepare employees for change, such as an internal communication campaign and a work survey.

With regard to efficiency and cost-reduction measures, Company 5 generally describes profitability as a key pillar of its seven strategic areas of action, but no major cost-reduction programs have been initialized and emphasized in the communications toward investors recently. In contrast to the other four case companies, Company 5 does not show a particularly strong effort in either growth or cost reduction. The statements and publications suggest a rather balanced strategy, which is overall in line with the initiatives discussed regarding the digitization of management accounting.

5.7.6 Discussion of Relation of Strategy to the Digitization of Management Accounting

As stated earlier (see Section 2), literature suggests that links exist between particular types of strategy and individual management accounting practices, in which strategy is described as a contextual variable of management accounting systems (Gerdin & Greve, 2004; Guilding, 1999; Lachmann et al., 2013; Langfield-Smith, 1997). Hence, one could assume that there is also a link between the digitization of management accounting (which potentially changes management accounting practices, processes, and tools) and the strategy of the firm (Chenhall, 2003; Lachmann et al., 2013; Quattrone & Hopper, 2005).

Digitization efforts in management accounting fit into the overall strategy and are in line with what the companies have announced regarding their strategic focus. However, when a bottom-up or mixed change approach is applied, the link to strategy is more predominant or visible (as, for example, in Company 4) than in the top-down approach (as, for example, in Company 1). As shown in Company 1, a cost-focus strategy is not as strongly covered in strategic publications as it was stressed in the interviews of this study. As previously outlined, the strategies can be generally described as those of cost leadership, differentiation, and focus (Joannidès de Lautour, 2018; McGahan & Porter, 2002; Montgomery & Porter, 1991; Porter, 1985). Referring to these strategies and to the archetypes of change (see Section 5.6), one can conclude that there is, indeed, a link between the respective strategies and management accounting digitization.

5.8 Analyzing a (Potentially) Futuristic View on Management Accounting: Perspective of Software Providers

As shown in Fig. 5.3, representatives of four different software providers were interviewed. Software providers and management accounting have an interdependent relationship. For software providers, it is critical to understand the challenges their clients are facing to develop the most suitable products and solutions. Software providers can (in cooperation with the management accountants) drive change and innovation in management accounting with their solutions. Thus, it is important to incorporate their perspective in this study in an attempt to better understand the potential characteristics of the future of management accounting digitization.

The interviews with software providers showed that, in general, their view on the digitization of management accounting is indeed pointed toward the future. These forward-looking stakeholders tend to try to think in innovative ways to address present challenges as well as to improve their services and products in a competitive market. Disruption and innovation are two themes that dominate the discussions in the interviews, especially when compared to the views of management accountants in the case companies. With a large number of clients, software companies are able to provide different standpoint which is less affected by the situation of one company. Because they aim to sell solutions to management accounting and finance teams, software providers apply their views on how management accounting could develop. To some extent, the software providers can push developments by focusing on certain technologies or topics. However, one should also consider that their view on what their technology can do might be optimistic because it is developed by them and because to some extend, they are aiming to sell it. However, overall, the perspective (which differs from the other perspectives covered in the case companies) enriched the view on management accounting digitization for the factors mentioned above.

Four software providers were interviewed. All the case companies are using large providers as their one-stop-shop for their management accounting teams. Large software providers offer a broad set of solutions covering everything from ERP to data mining. Among the selected software providers, some are specialists that provide software for specific (management accounting) tasks, such as planning. These specialized players provided their view of the task changes as well as where they believe the future of management accounting is heading. However, larger providers tend to have a more holistic overview of the management accounting function and how it is being impacted by digitization.

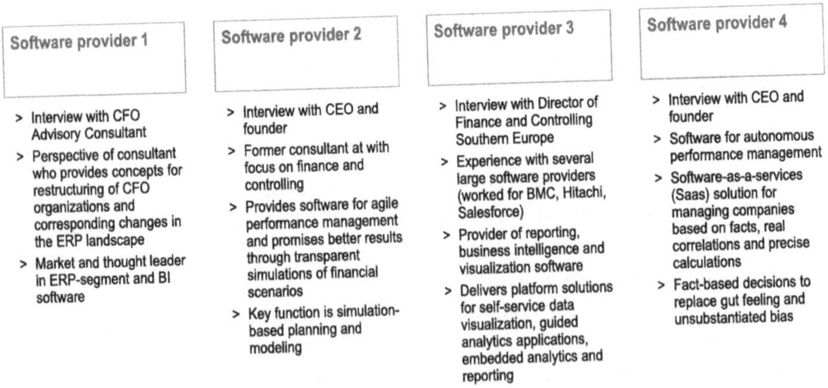

Fig. 5.3 Interviews with software providers

5.8.1 View on RQ1

As mentioned in the introduction, the perspective of software providers was considered to gain a more future-oriented view on the research questions. When interpreting the statements of the interviewees, the fact that they are also biased to some degree has been considered because these interviewees are employed by software companies that aim to sell new software.

With regard to the tasks of management accounting, software providers have a more critical view of the needs of management accounting employees (in the way they work today). Software providers see, for instance, a higher potential for automation when it comes to management accounting: "*Automation will certainly eliminate many of the areas of management accounting that you have today. That is, if you have an automated production controlling at 90 percent, let's assume that these functionalities will effectively disappear*" (CFO Consultant, Software Provider 4). To some extent, automation is expected to positively impact the work of management accountants because manual work effort is reduced and, thus, mistakes are reduced as well. Combined with machine learning, automation can also lead to transactions that are conducted without human interactions. This would also reduce manual effort. Automation is also leveraged in shared service centers, resulting in the need for fewer resources to conduct the same processes faster.

However, software providers also field critical questions with regard to the future of employees: "*Where do we need accounting, audit, treasury employees in the future? This is what customers often ask us. In my opinion, one should look at it from a positive aspect that the employees can focus on the more complex, interesting tasks of supporting really important decisions and being able to let the machine do the boring, repetitive tasks*" (CFO Consultant, Software Provider 4). A higher degree of automation might result in "*[f]ast decision-making [as a result of] having accounting and controlling data in real time available*" (CEO, Software Provider 1). Simulation is expected to be one major trend in management accounting: "*More predictive analytics and simulations of different scenarios can help to have a better future outlook*" (Director, Software Provider 3).

Machine learning and artificial intelligence, which have been applied only to a limited extent by the case companies, are expected by software providers to have a higher impact in the short term: "*Machine learning will help in several ways in management accounting and related fields. They can help to recognize patterns and correlations in transactional processes and also avoid mistakes [through] adjustments of the algorithms. With regard to forecasts, I expect machine learning to push the quality of forecasts further, which will help management accounting*" (CFO Consultant, Software Provider 4). Another major technology that is expected to impact management accounting is mobile technology. Software companies see mobile solutions as enablers for "*informed decision-making anytime and real-time reporting and analysis*" (CFO Consultant, Software Provider 4). Additionally, mobile technology could help management accountants grow in their advisory role because it enables "*better communication with the business*" (CEO, Software Provider 2). Finally, it is also regarded as an enabler for the further increase of "*self-service management accounting and, hence, helps to reduce the workload of the management accounting function*" (Director, Software Provider 3).

5.8.2 View on RQ2

Software providers expect the size of management accounting teams to decrease due to higher automation of repetitive tasks like reporting. This applies especially to local management accounting units. Software providers expect management accountants to instead "*be the interface between the business, IT, and finance*" (CFO Consultant, Software Provider 4). Management accountants are expected to focus further on the advisory role and, hence, must ensure their ability to fulfill this role by organizationally securing a close position to management.

Interviewees from the case companies believe that software providers see the importance of shared service centers. However, in the long run, software companies expect these jobs to be automated to a degree that does not require large numbers of employees in shared centers for management accounting: "*[The] profitability of the shared service center has not been proven, in my view. I see them much more as preparation toward automation, especially when it comes to [the] standardization of IT landscapes and processes*" (CEO, Software Provider 2).

Correspondingly, the organizational option to outsource teams is expected to be less attractive in the future because the tasks that can be outsourced today are mostly repetitive. These might be automated to a large extent: "*In the long run, management accounting should only deal with tasks directly related to supporting business decisions. In that case, outsourcing is not an option anymore.... [T]oday, outsourcing takes place only for tasks that are ... very repetitive and, in the future, will be taken over by machines*" (CEO, Software Provider 1).

5.8.3 View on RQ3

Corresponding with the changes in tasks expected for management accounting, slightly adjusted skill sets are expected from management accountants. A certain level of data literacy is also important from the viewpoint of software providers. However, skills that go further and cover, for instance, coding proficiency are not necessary for every management accountant. According to the software providers, it proves beneficial, however, if the management accountant understands basic coding structures to be able to understand and interpret results provided by algorithms. Overall, an improved level of IT skills and a strong cooperation with the IT function is expected in the future: "*[A] management accountant is like a pilot, who must understand how to fly a plane, who knows where he can intervene if necessary, but who cannot master and understand the whole technology behind it. So, somewhere, there are limits*" (CEO, Software Provider 2).

According to the software providers, the challenge could be to develop management accountants from the role of conducting simple tasks like creating Excel files on demand toward an advisory role: "*[The] focus will be on [an] advisory [role], hence, ... communication skills and a good business understanding are expected to play a bigger role. Management accountants supporting managers, [such as] sales managers, should also be eligible to join meetings with clients. This requires different skills than what was required in the past*" (Director, Software Provider 3).

5.9 Conclusions from Findings

The findings suggest that there are differences between the selected case companies in terms of how they have been impacted by digitization and how various companies have reacted to the change.

New technologies and ideas are being introduced; however, the management accounting function is still in transformation and more disruptive changes are expected by interviewees. The two archetypes that emerged indicate that most of the companies focus on either reducing costs through digitization or on strengthening growth efforts with the help of digital analytics.

In the future, companies are expected to continue to develop a holistic concept and strategy regarding the digitization of management accounting. As of now, the landscape is rather scattered, and although pilot projects such as the investigation of artificial intelligence for data analysis have been introduced as the first step to a wider transformation, measures have not been rolled out across the whole organization. This study revealed that training activities are necessary to ensure management accountants have the required skills. The potential for technological improvements, such as artificial intelligence, has also been discussed. However, those solutions are currently limited in their implementation. Software providers project that there can be more expected in the near future.

The case studies also prove that there are opportunities and challenges for management accounting under digitization. There are indications that management accountants can help make better decisions that are based on facts with the improved ability to process larger datasets as well as through more robust analyses for decision preparation. However, there are also challenges for management accounting. Under digitization, tasks conducted by management accounting today have been or will be automated, and if management accountants do not develop themselves and their role further, their jobs might be at risk. Hence, the challenge will be to develop the skill sets that will enable management accountants of the future to advise management on crucial decisions.

5.10 Discussion of Findings

Overall, the implementation of new tools and processes are ongoing but do not yet penetrate the whole management accounting function of the case companies. Relating the findings back to the two theoretical perspectives (organizational and individual), one can see how the current strategic focus impacts the digitization of management accounting. The role of management accounting is interpreted very differently in cost-reduction situations than in situations in which companies focus on growth and diversification. From the analysis, one cannot clearly distinguish the case companies as applying a pure cost or diversification strategy as described by Porter (1985). However, one can say that if the overall focus is on costs and streamlining, the companies tend to place less value on additional services provided by management accountants. These companies tend to see management accounting rather as a cost factor. In contrast, in a diversification and growth situation, companies seek to use management accounting as a facilitator to provide analyses and information on how to grow revenues. The way management accountants work with digitization is thus influenced by the current overall strategic focus of the company.

The introduction of shared service centers and the standardization of processes have been referred to within the theoretical concept of division of labor and the objective to achieve economies of scope and scale in terms of costs (as first described by Henderson, 1968). Companies introduce shared service centers to reduce labor costs through specialization and the bundling of expertise in one location. Although the shared service centers are established mostly in low-cost countries, the main benefit is achieved due to economies of scope and scale rather than from lower wages and salaries. With regard to the concepts discussed in the individual perspective, one can also tell from the interviews that individuals (especially management accountants) aim to position their function in a way that ensures the relevance and importance of management accounting in the future, such as pushing for increased data analytics capabilities in the management accounting function rather than sourcing services internally from another function in which data analytics skills could be bundled for the whole firm.

With regard to heuristics and biases (based on Tversky and Kahneman, 1974), the decrease in errors due to the reduction of human manual work stood out. The majority of the management accountants interviewed welcome the introduction of automation and the opportunity it offers in reducing the likelihood of errors, such as in compiling reports automatically from an ERP system rather than having to manually collect data prone to human errors. In addition, the managers as internal clients of management accountants and the management accountants themselves argued that digitization could help prevent bias in the decisions made in a firm by basing them on objective figures and trends rather than the subjective feelings or opinions of decision-makers. However, the trend towards self-reporting also entails the risk of new biases because managers could be tempted to use self-reporting tools in a way which favors their gut-based decisions. Since the controlling counterpart from the management accountant is not involved anymore, this could lead to decisions which are again biased. This way of thought can be linked back to Social Exchange Theory (Blau, 1964; Homans, 1958) as described in the individual perspective of the theory section.

Taking into consideration the literature reviewed, it is clear that the practitioner's articles reflect the status of digitization of management accounting to a much broader extent than the studies published in academic journals. As discussed in some of the recent articles, this leads to the same belief that is often brought up by management accountants: the discussion of the direction and purpose of research in management accounting is deemed necessary because it does not seem to focus on the topics regarded as crucial and relevant by practitioners. Practitioners argue that research on management accounting currently focuses on concepts and questions that are too theoretical and distant from the work of management accountants to be beneficial.

6 Conclusion

6.1 Summary

In this summary, crucial points of this study are reviewed and concluded. The motivation to conduct this study stems from an academic but also practical interest of the author of management accounting digitization from his studies and work as a management consultant. A perceived gap in research and knowledge in practice led the author to take on this research endeavor. Based on the motivation and interest, a literature review was conducted to define the state of research in the field of management accounting digitization. The literature review shed further light on the existing research gap of in-depth empirical studies at the interface of digitization and management accounting. Although selected studies exist, the majority either focus on a single aspect or do not conduct empirical work to test claims made by the authors.

Theories were then analyzed to learn to what extent they could help frame the research and explain potential findings. During the empirical work and the analysis of the interviews, the author switched between theory and findings to make further sense of the data.

Finally, a theoretical framework to explain the measures of the organizations and the motivation and behavior of individuals was derived. The organizational perspective is based on the concept of the division of labor (Smith, 1778) and Porter's (1985) generic strategies to explain how management, as an agent of the company, aims to digitalize the management accounting function. The individual perspective, on the other hand, points out the potential behavior of individuals regarding the digitization of management accounting, referring to social exchange theory and to

O. Holtkemper, *Digitization of the Management Accounting Function*, Controlling und Rechnungslegung – Managerial and Financial Accounting, https://doi.org/10.1007/978-3-658-31509-2_6

the impact of the human mind on decision-making, based on work from Tversky and Kahneman (1974).

Based on the early state of the phenomenon and the few empirical studies conducted, a qualitative research framework using case studies was adopted because there is a lack of a sufficient theoretical basis and prior research for a quantitative study. Explorative case studies help in gaining a better understanding of the phenomenon and backing it up with data. The cases for the study were carefully selected based on criteria such as the size, sector, and geographical setup of the organizations. Five cases were selected and 28 interviews were conducted.

One of the major findings of the study is the identification of two archetypes of digitization in management accounting. The five case companies are scattered along the two axes, upon which two archetypes of management accounting digitization have emerged. One of the case companies conducts a streamlining (top-down) approach, whereas three other companies apply an enabling (bottom-up) approach. Only one of the case companies apply a wide mix of bottom-up and top-down measures to tackle the digitization of management accounting.

To make further sense of the archetypes, the companies' overall situations and strategies were considered. Interestingly, the author discovered that in growth strategies, management accounting is involved in making appropriate decisions, whereas in cost-reduction and streamlining situations, management accounting is considered one of many cost factors that can be further automated. Hence, although management accounting can (as prior research suggests) provide support in implementing strategies and providing analyses to improve cost measures, it is also affected by cost-reduction measures, as are other functions. One could conclude from this finding that the real added value of management accounting is only recognized in situations of growth.

As shown in Company 3, another valuable finding from this study is that a shift in company strategy also affects management accounting and, thus, how it is impacted by digitization. If growth cannot be realized and supported by management accounting, cost reductions also are applied heavily on it. Also, investments, such as the test phase of a big data team previously established, are reduced.

Overall, further innovation and a push for digitization are expected. As the interviews with software providers have shown, they are expected to push for new technologies and further application of existing technologies. With regard to what degree the digitization of management accounting has progressed, the findings of this study suggest that the focus is still on standardizing tasks and tools. New technologies like artificial intelligence are partly tested but not yet applied on a broad scale. Management accountants and related functions have recognized the need to develop the function further toward value-added advisory services for decision-makers.

Comparing the theoretical framework and the findings from the interviews, one can see that the contrast of the individual and organizational perspectives plays a role. From the organizational perspective, the strategies derived by Porter (1985) can have a significant impact on the digitization of management accounting. Also, the interviews proved that the individual management accountants are trying to shape solutions that benefit them the most. The same applies to internal customers who aim to receive improved services from management accounting. Hence, in this exchange of ideas, aspects of social exchange theory become obvious because all perspectives aim to maximize their own benefit. This study adds to the theory on the complex phenomenon of digitization in management accounting by deriving archetypes of digitization and setting those theories applied in the framework into the context of the changes investigated in the empirical work.

Hence, as stated earlier, the major contributions of this study to the literature in the field of management accounting can be summarized as follows:

1. *Framework*: The study provides a framework through which to analyze the impact of digitization on management accounting.
2. *Empirical evidence*: It is one of the first studies to provide empirical evidence on the impact of management accounting digitization based on detailed case studies and interviews with practitioners.
3. *Triangulation of perspectives*: The triangulation of perspectives within the cases through interviewing not just management accountants and experts from the field but also enablers (i.e., IT and HR) and internal customers (e.g., sales managers and production managers) ensures that not only the management accountants' views are covered but also those of other functions involved. Hence, biases and subjectivity can be reduced. This is the first study to apply this approach to the field of digitization of management accounting.
4. *Derivation of archetypes*: Based on the framework and the empirical work, archetypes of digitization in management accounting were derived. Additional empirical work in the future can build upon the archetypes and, for instance, could further test them in a quantitative study.
5. *International applicability*: This study can be helpful on a broad basis because findings are not limited to one country or one industrial sector because all the case companies have international operations and are based in various manufacturing industries, such as pharmaceuticals, mechanical engineering, chemicals, consumer goods, and automotive suppliers. In contrast to previous studies that partly focus on one industry or geographical background, these findings contribute to research on a broader set of industries and countries.

6.2 Practical Implications

In addition to contributing to scientific progress in a comparatively new field, this study also seeks to provide insights, implications, and recommendations for the practical work of management accountants.

Based on the research, several implications can be derived. One is that the digitization of management accounting is more of an opportunistic initiative rather than a conceptual strategy for the whole function. For management accounting to maintain its importance, it is crucial to develop a vision for itself for the future within a company and provide ideas and measures that will add to the value of a company. Therefore, a holistic approach that takes into consideration the differences between functions is imperative. Cross-functional cooperation is key in maximizing the benefits of digitization. The degree of repetitive tasks compared to more complex tasks of a function should also be taken into consideration because complex tasks are harder to automate than repetitive, simple tasks.

Following a "one solution fits all" approach might reduce headcount and costs across various functions in the short run but, in the long run, might have negative effects if important functions such as management accounting, which provides decision support, must reduce personnel for a short-term benefit. For example, companies may not benefit from the increased data gathered if there are fewer employees to analyze it.

At the moment, there is still not enough incentive and alertness to prepare all functions for digitization. Awareness needs to be raised further, especially with top management members, without which they fail to provide solutions and concepts to develop employees and prepare them for digitization. Key personnel such as chief HR officers should be highly alert and start implementing measures to ensure that the organization is well-equipped to take full advantage of digitization.

For management accounting to bolster its role in companies, group leaders and employees must strengthen their ties to top management and underline their value for decision support. Management accountants need to ensure that they bolster their service to internal clients—if the value-add is no longer visible or if tasks are taken over by other functions, it could have drastic consequences for management accounting. Management accountants must be able to provide a valuable service for internal customers, fulfilling tasks that are important and useful to them. Otherwise, further reduction of resources and teams could follow.

Management accountants also need to position themselves better within the company. By aligning themselves closer to the specialist functions, they can ensure that value-add is created for their clients. At the same time, close collaboration with IT is important for them to benefit from new applications and tools that further increase the value-add of management accounting for decision-makers and other stakeholders within the firm. Applications and tools should enable management accountants to provide additional information and knowledge to decision-makers.

Under cost-reduction circumstances, rather than assessing the value-add and information that management accounting can provide, companies tend to apply similar cost-cutting measures to all the functions. In these situations, management accounting should argue in favor of its value proposition, which should be viewed and assessed separately from other functions and not be treated as a normal cost position with a proportional cost-reduction target (i.e., reducing headcount).

Another crucial measure to better prepare management accountants is to develop roles and corresponding skill profiles. This is a task not just for management accounting but one that should be accompanied by the support of HR. Because it is applicable to more than just the management accounting function, HR should proactively assume an active role in preparing employees for digitization and shaping the future of the work of the functions affected by digitization. This can allow the company to gain a competitive advantage rather than waiting for the situation to reach a critical point at which a reaction is unavoidable.

Across the case companies, we see a need for the continuous education of employees because software solutions and technology in general change rapidly. Whereas the change in the past was very slow—for instance, Microsoft Excel was a standard solution used for decades—in the future, faster and more disruptive innovation in the field of technology for management accounting is expected.

In terms of organization, shared service centers are gaining importance in the digitization process. Although the introduction of shared service centers has been occurring for more than a decade, the speed of change and the change in the role of shared service centers needs to be considered. Tasks are bundled in shared service centers, standardized, and then automated to a high degree. Companies need to consider that knowledge of processes and tasks is also shifting toward shared service centers. Also, if the plan is to automate tasks within the shared service centers, expertise on those tasks and on the automation of processes needs to be developed in those centers.

6.3 Limitations of Study and Suggestions for Further Research

During this research project, the author followed a strict methodological guideline. However, as for every research project, there are still limitations to the findings presented. Although several perspectives were covered for all cases, it was not possible to create a complete picture in the study's timeframe, as it would involve much broader and in-depth interview sessions with every department. Hence, when interpreting and using the results for further studies, this limitation should be considered. Furthermore, as is the case with all interview-based studies, to some degree, findings can be biased due to the subjective information provided by the interviewees. Nevertheless, measures were implemented to reduce biases by including several perspectives and conducting interviews separately whenever feasible. Although all case companies are operating internationally, the fact that all interviewees were based in Europe could have biased the information because their perceptions of digitization could differ from those of management accountants located in other regions, such as the United States or Asia. With regard to the industries covered, the focus of this study is on manufacturing companies, which makes it difficult to draw conclusions for management accounting in general, although there might be a high correlation in the digitization of management accounting in, for instance, the financial services sector.

The overarching aim of this study was to gain knowledge on the digitization of management accounting, upon which management accountants and researchers in the field can develop future works. Specifically, this qualitative study aimed to provide initial explorative research on the impact of management accounting digitization in manufacturing companies. The implications explored in this study could be used for a quantitative study that tests the findings using a larger set of manufacturing companies. The findings described in this multiple case study could also be analyzed quantitatively by surveying a larger set of management accounting professionals in manufacturing companies. Furthermore, the relationship between the strategic situation of a company and the way the digitization of management accounting is conducted could be tested using a larger set of companies. A quantitative study could also elaborate on the archetypes described and find out how, in a representative set of companies, the number of companies compares regarding the bottom-up, top-down, and mixed approaches.

Another valuable way to build on the findings would be to conduct a comparable study with non-manufacturing companies to compare different sectors. For instance, management accounting in the financial services industry could provide different insights. The same applies to the size of the case companies. Research with smaller companies could shed light on the difference the size of a company makes with regard to the questions discussed. In addition, the impact of different origins of the company could be researched. For instance, companies with their headquarters in Asia might deal differently with the challenge of the digitization of their management accounting function. Another interesting and influential aspect could be the ownership structure of the companies, which could lead to different approaches and foci in terms of implementing digital solutions.

As the findings of this study indicate, in management accounting functions, employees are not being prepared sufficiently with the right skills and knowledge. Studies on how universities and other educational institutions approach the challenge could prove helpful not just for research but also for practitioners.

Further research could also consider enlarging this methodology into a longitudinal study by conducting interviews of the same nature in the future and comparing the status of today with those new findings. By doing so, researchers could evaluate whether the expectations mentioned in this study regarding the future of the management accounting function hold true.

Bibliography

Ahmed, N. (2008). Financial Accounting – A Simplified Approach, 3.

Akter, S., Wamba, S. F., Gunasekaran, A., Dubey, R., & Childe, S. J. (2016). How to improve firm performance using big data analytics capability and business strategy alignment? *International Journal of Production Economics, 182*, 113–131.

Al-Htaybat, K., & von Alberti-Alhtaybat, L. (2017). Big data and corporate reporting: Impacts and paradoxes. *Accounting, Auditing & Accountability Journal, 30* (4), 850–873.

Armitage, H. M., Webb, A., & Glynn, J. (2016). The use of management accounting techniques by small and medium-sized enterprises: A field study of Canadian and Australian practice. *Accounting Perspectives, 15* (1), 31–69.

Arnaboldi, M., Busco, C., & Cuganesan, S. (2017). Accounting, accountability, social media and big data. Revolution or hype? *Accounting, Auditing & Accountability Journal, 30* (4), 762–776.

Ax, C., & Greve, J. (2016). Adoption of management accounting innovations: Organizational culture compatibility and perceived outcomes. *Management Accounting Research, 34*, 59–74.

Baldwin, A. A., Brown, C. E., & Trinkle, B. S. (2006). Opportunities for artificial intelligence development in the accounting domain: The case for auditing. *Intelligent Systems in Accounting, Finance and Management, 14* (3), 77–86.

Beaman, I., & Richardson, B. (2007). Information technology, decision support and management accounting roles. *Journal of Applied Management Accounting Research, 5* (1).

Bhimani, A. (2003). *Management accounting in the digital economy*. New York: Oxford University Press.

Bhimani, A. (Ed.). (2006a). *Contemporary issues in management accounting*. New York: Oxford University Press.

Bhimani, A. (2006b). Management accounting and digitization. In A. Bhimani (Ed.), *Contemporary issues in management accounting* (pp. 69–91). New York: Oxford University Press.

Bhimani, A., & Bromwich, M. (2009). Management accounting in a digital and global economy: The interface of strategy, technology, and cost information. In C. S. Chapman, D.

O. Holtkemper, *Digitization of the Management Accounting Function*, Controlling und Rechnungslegung – Managerial and Financial Accounting, https://doi.org/10.1007/978-3-658-31509-2

J. Cooper, & P. Miller (Eds.), *Accounting, organizations, and institutions* (85–111). New York: Oxford University Press.

Bhimani, A., & Langfield-Smith, K. (2007). Structure, formality and the importance of financial and non-financial information in strategy development and implementation. *Management Accounting Research, 18* (1), 3–31.

Bhimani, A., & Willcocks, L. (2014). Digitisation, 'Big Data' and the transformation of accounting information. *Accounting and Business Research, 44* (4), 469–490.

Blau, P. M. (1964). *Exchange and power in social life.* New York: John Wiley & Sons.

Booth, P., Matolcsy, Z., & Wieder, B. (2000). The impacts of enterprise resource planning systems on accounting practice: The Australian experience. *Australian Accounting Review, 10* (22), 4–18.

Brandas, C., Megan, O., & Didraga, O. (2015). Global perspectives on accounting information systems: Mobile and cloud approach. *Procedia Economics and Finance, 20,* 88–93.

Brennen, J. S. & Kreiss, D. (2016): Digitalization, In: Jensen, K., Craig, R. T., Pooley, J. & Rothenbuhler, E. W., The international encyclopedia of communication theory and philosophy, First published, 556–566.

Bromwich, M. (1990). The case for strategic management accounting: The role of accounting information for strategy in competitive markets. *Accounting, Organizations and Society, 15* (1–2), 27–46.

Burns, J., Quinn, M., Warren, L., & Oliveira, J. (2013). *Management accounting.* London: McGraw-Hill.

Chapman, C. S., Cooper, D. J., & Miller, P. (Eds.). (2009). *Accounting, organizations, and institutions.* New York: Oxford University Press.

Chenhall, R. H. (2003). Management control systems design within its organizational context: Findings from contingency-based research and directions for the future. *Accounting, Organizations and Society, 28* (2/3), 127–168.

Chenhall, R. H., & Langfield-Smith, K. (1998). The relationship between strategic priorities, management techniques and management accounting: An empirical investigation using a systems approach. *Accounting, Organizations and Society, 23* (3), 243–264.

Chartered Institute of Management Accountants (CIMA). (2005). CIMA Official Terminology. Amsterdam: Elsevier Science.

Choe, J.-M. (2002). The organizational learning effects of management accounting information under advanced manufacturing technology. *European Journal of Information Systems, 11* (2), 142–158.

Coakley, J. R., & Brown, C. E. (2000). Artificial neural networks in accounting and finance: Modeling issues. *Intelligence Systems in Accounting, Finance & Management, 9* (2), 119–144.

Corbin, J., & Strauss, A. (2008). *Basics of qualitative research: Techniques and procedures for developing grounded theory* (3rd ed.). Thousand Oaks, CA: Sage Publications, Inc.

Daft, R. L. (2016). *Organization theory & design* (12th ed.). Boston, MA: Cengage Learning.

De Vaus, D. A. (2014). Surveys in Social Research. (6th ed). Australia: UCL Press, 6.

Denzin, N., & Lincoln, Y. (1998). Entering the field of qualitative research. In N. Denzin & Y. Lincoln (Eds.), Collecting and interpreting qualitative materials. London: Sage, 1–34.

Eisenhardt, K. M. (1989). Building theories from case study research. *Academy of Management Review, 14* (4), 532–550.

Feldman, T. (1997). *An introduction to digital media.* New York: Routledge, 1–21.

Fullerton, R. R., Kennedy, F. A., & Widener, S. K. (2013). Management accounting and control practices in a lean manufacturing environment. *Accounting, Organizations and Society, 38* (1), 50–71.

Gamage, P. (2016): Big Data: are accounting educators ready? Accounting and Management Information Systems, *15 (3), 588–604.*

Gerdin, J., & Greve, J. (2004). Forms of contingency fit in management accounting research: A critical review. *Accounting, Organizations and Society, 29* (3/4), 303–326.

Glaser, B. G., & Strauss, A. L. (1967): *The discovery of grounded theory*. Chicago: Aldine.

Granlund, M., & Lukka, K. (1998). It's a small world of management accounting practices. *Journal of Management Accounting Research, 10,* 153–179.

Grothe, M. (2016). Early detection of threats, risks, issues, and talents on the Internet: Hypothesis-free and in real time (in German). *Controlling, 28* (3), 166–173.

Guilding, C. (1999). Competitor-focused accounting: An exploratory note. *Accounting, Organizations and Society, 24* (7), 583–595.

Guilding, C., Cravens, K. S., & Tayles, M. (2000). An international comparison of strategic management accounting practices. *Management Accounting Research, 11* (1), 113–135.

Güney, A. (2014). Role of technology in accounting and e-accounting. *Procedia, Social and Behavioral Sciences, 152,* 852–855.

Helgesen, Ø. (2007). Customer accounting and customer profitability analysis for the order handling industry: A managerial accounting approach. *Industrial Marketing Management, 36* (6), 757–769.

Henderson, B. (1968). Perspectives on experience. Boston, MA: The Boston Consulting Group.

Hoffjan, A. (2008). Comparative management accounting: Vergleich des anglo-amerikanischen management accounting und des deutschen controllings (in German). *Controlling, 20* (12), 655–661.

Homans, G. C. (1958). *Social behavior as exchange.* American Journal of Sociology, 63: 597–606.

Horngren, C. T., Datar, S. M., & Rajan, M. V. (2013). *Cost accounting: A managerial emphasis* (14th ed.). Upper Saddle River, NJ: Pearson/Prentice Hall.

Horngren, C. T., Sundem, G.L.,Stratton, W.O., Burgstahler, D. & Schatzberg, J. (2008): Introduction to management accounting. Upper Saddle River, NJ: Pearson Prentice Hall, 5.

Jämsä-Jounela, S.-L. (2007). Future trends in process automation. *Annual Reviews in Control, 31* (2), 211–220.

Janvrin, D. J., & Weidenmier Watson, M. (2017). "Big Data": A new twist to accounting. *Journal of Accounting Education, 38,* 3–8.

Jarvenpaa, S. L., & Lang, K. R. (2005). Managing the paradoxes of mobile technology. *Information Systems Management, 22* (4), 7–23.

Jeacle, I., & Carter, C. (2011). In TripAdvisor we trust: Rankings, calculative regimes and abstract systems. *Accounting, Organizations and Society, 36* (4), 293–309.

Jensen, M. C., & Meckling, W. H. (1976). Theory of the firm: Managerial behavior, agency costs and ownership structure. Journal of financial economics, 3(4), 305–360.

Joannidès de Lautour, V. (2018). *Strategic management accounting, Volume I: Aligning strategy, operations and finance*. London: Palgrave Macmillan.

Katz, R. & Koutroumpis, P. (2013). "*Measuring digitization: A growth and welfare multiplier*", Technovation, 33, 314–319.

Kaye, G. R., & Nicholson, A.H.S. (1992). An educational framework for information technology in accounting and management education. *Computers & Education, 19* (1–2), 105–112.

Kelton, A. S., & Pennington, R. R. (2012). Internet financial reporting: The effects of information presentation format and content differences on investor decision making. *Computers in Human Behavior, 28* (4), 1178–1185.

Kolbjørnsrud, V., Amico, R., & Thomas, R. J. (2016). How artificial intelligence will redefine management. *Harvard Business Review*. Retrieved from https://hbr.org/2016/11/how-artificial-intelligence-will-redefine-management.

Lachmann, M., & Holtkemper, O. (2021). Strategische Archetypen der Digitalisierung im Controlling – Empirische Erkenntnisse aus Fallstudien in Großunternehmen. *Zeitschrift für Controlling*, forthcoming.

Lachmann, M., Knauer, T., & Trapp, R. (2013). Strategic management accounting practices in hospitals. *Journal of Accounting & Organizational Change, 9* (3), 336–369.

Lachmann, M., & Wenger, F. (2012). Dashboards. *Controlling, 24* (12), 715.

Langfield-Smith, K. (1997). Management control systems and strategy: A critical review. *Accounting, Organizations and Society, 22* (2), 207–232.

Leedy, P., & Ormrod, J. E. (2014). *Practical research planning and design* (10th ed.). Edinburgh: Pearson Educational Inc.

Mancini, D., Dameri, R. P., & Bonollo, E. (2016). *Strengthening information and control systems: The synergy between information technology and accounting models* (p. 14). Switzerland: Springer International Publishing.

Maxwell, J. A. (2013). *Qualitative research design: An interactive approach*. Thousand Oaks, CA: Sage Publications.

McGahan, A. M., & Porter, M. E. (2002). What do we know about variance in accounting profitability? *Management Science, 48* (7), 834–851.

Marchant, G. (2013): *Management Accounting in the 21st Century: A Profession for Which the Time Has Come, Journal of Applied Management Accounting Research, 13 (2).*

Merchant, K. A., & van der Stede, W. A. (2017). *Management control systems: Performance measurement, evaluation, and incentives* (4th ed.). Harlow, England: Pearson.

Miles, M. B., & Huberman, A. M. (1994). *Qualitative data analysis: An expanded sourcebook* (2nd ed.). Thousand Oaks, CA/London: Sage.

Moll, J., Major, M., & Hoque, Z. (2006). The qualitative research tradition. In Z. Hoque (Ed.), *Methodological issues in accounting research: Theories and methods* (pp. 375–398). London: Spiramus Press.

Montgomery, C. A., & Porter, M. E. (1991). *Strategy: Seeking and securing competitive advantage*. Cambridge, MA: Harvard University Press.

Moorthy, M. K., Voon, O. O., Samsuri, C.A.S., Gopalan, M., & Yew, K. T. (2012). Application of information technology in management accounting decision making. *International Journal of Academic Research in Business and Social Sciences*, 2 (3), 1–16.

Nyamori, R. O., Perera, M.H.B., & Lawrence, S. R. (2001). The concept of strategic change and implications for management accounting research. *Journal of Accounting Literature, 20*, 62–83.

O'Brien, T. (2015). 'Accounting' for data quality in enterprise systems. *Procedia Computer Science, 64*, 442–449.

Pan, G., & Seow, P.-S. (2016). Preparing accounting graduates for digital revolution: A critical review of information technology competencies and skills development. *Journal of Education for Business, 91* (3), 166–175.

Parker, L., & Langfield-Smith, K. (2008). Strategic management accounting: How far have we come in 25 years? *Accounting, Auditing & Accountability Journal, 21* (2), 204–228.

Patton, M. Q. (1987). *How to use qualitative methods in evaluation* (Program evaluation kit, 2nd ed.). Newbury Park, CA: Sage Publications.

Peral, J. Maté, A. and Marco,M. (2017): A*pplication of Data Mining techniques to identify relevant Key Performance Indicators*, Computer Standards & Interfaces.

Peters, M. D., Wieder, B., Sutton, S. G., & Wakefield, J. (2016). Business intelligence systems use in performance measurement capabilities: Implications for enhanced competitive advantage. *International Journal of Accounting Information Systems, 21*, 1–17.

Phillips, P., & Halliday, S. V. (2008): Marketing/accounting synergy: A discussion of its potential and evidence in e-business planning. *Journal of Marketing Management, 24* (7–8), 751–770.

Porter, M. E. (1985). *The competitive advantage: Creating and sustaining superior performance.* New York: Free Press.

Porter, M. E. (1998). *Competitive advantage: Creating and sustaining superior performance.* Cambridge, MA: Harvard University Press.

Prendergast, C. (1999). "The Provision of Incentives in Firms." Journal of Economic Literature. XXXVII, 7–63.

Quattrone, P. (2016). Management accounting goes digital: Will the move make it wiser? *Management Accounting Research, 31*, 118–122.

Quattrone, P., & Hopper, T. (2005). A "time-space odyssey": Management control systems in two multinational organizations. *Accounting, Organizations and Society, 30* (7/8), 735–764.

Ramli, I., & Iskandar, D. (2014). Control authority, business strategy, and the characteristics of management accounting information systems. *Procedia Social and Behavioral Sciences, 164*, 384–390.

Robinson, O. C. (2014). Sampling in interview-based qualitative research: A theoretical and practical guide. *Qualitative Research in Psychology*, I (1), 25–41.

Rom, A., & Rohde, C. (2007). Management accounting and integrated information systems: A literature review. *International Journal of Accounting Information Systems, 8* (1), 40–68.

Samad, T., McLaughlin, P., & Lu, J. (2007). System architecture for process automation: Review and trends. *Journal of Process Control, 17* (3), 191–201.

Scott, S. V., & Orlikowski, W. J. (2012). Reconfiguring relations of accountability: Materialization of social media in the travel sector. *Accounting, Organizations and Society, 37* (1), 26–40.

Sheridan, T. (1995). Management accounting in global European corporations: Anglophone and continental viewpoints. *Management Accounting Research, 6* (3), 287–294.

Shields, M. D. (1998). Management accounting practices in Europe: A perspective from the States. *Management Accounting Research, 9* (4), 501–513.

Silvestre, J. (1987). Economies and diseconomies of scale. In *The New Palgrave Dictionary of Economics, Vol. 2* (pp. 80–84). London: Macmillan.

Singh Wahla, R. (2011). *Accounting terminology bulletins, number 1, review and résumé.* New York: American Institute of Accountants.
Sledgianowski, D., Gomaa, M., & Tan, C. (2017). Toward integration of Big Data, technology and information systems competencies into the accounting curriculum. *Journal of Accounting Education, 38*, 81–93.
Smith, A. (1778). *An inquiry into the nature and causes of the wealth of nations, Volume 1* (2nd ed.). London: W. Strahan and T. Cadell.
Smith, J. A., Flowers, P., & Larkin, M. (2009). *Interpretative phenomenological analysis: Theory, method and research.* London: Sage.
Spraakman, G., O'Grady, W., Askarany, D., & Akroyd, C. (2015). Employers' perceptions of information technology competency requirements for management accounting graduates. *Accounting Education, 24* (5), 403–422.
Strauss, A. L., & Corbin, J. M. (1998): Grounded Theory Research: Procedures, Canons, and Evaluative Criteria. Qualitative Sociology, 13 (1), 3–21.
Strauss, A. L., & Corbin, J. M. (1998). *Basics of qualitative research: Techniques and procedures for developing grounded theory* (2nd ed.). Thousand Oaks, CA: Sage.
Tabak, D. (1971). Digitalisation of control systems. *Computer-Aided Design, 3* (2), 13–18.
Taipaleenmäki, J., & Ikäheimo, S. (2013). On the convergence of management accounting and financial accounting: The role of information technology in accounting change. *International Journal of Accounting Information Systems, 14* (4), 321–348.
Talha, M., Raja, J. B., & Seetharaman, A. (2010). A new look at management accounting. *Journal of Applied Business Research, 26* (4).
Terai, K., Sawai, M., Sugiura, N., Izumi, N., & Yamaguchi, T. (2002). Business process semi-automation based on business model management. *Intelligent Systems in Accounting, Finance and Management, 11* (4), 215–234.
Tillmann, K., & Goddard, A. (2008). Strategic management accounting and sense-making in a multinational company. *Management Accounting Research, 19* (1), 80–102.
Trigo, A., Belfo, F., & Estébanez, R. P. (2014). Accounting information systems: The challenge of the real-time reporting. *Procedia Technology, 16*, 118–127.
Tversky, A., & Kahneman, D. (1972). Subjective probability: A judgment of representativeness. *Cognitive Psychology, 3* (3), 430–454.
Tversky, A., & Kahneman, D. (1973). Availability: A heuristic for judging frequency and probability. *Cognitive Psychology, 5* (2), 207–232.
Tversky, A., & Kahneman, D. (1974). Judgment under uncertainty: Heuristics and biases. Science, *185* (4157), 1124–1131.
van der Stede, W. A. (2016). Management accounting in context: Industry, regulation and informatics. *Management Accounting Research, 31*, 100–102.
Vroom, V. H. (1964). Work and motivation. San Francisco, CA: Jossey-Bass.
Webb, E., & Weick, K. E. (1979). Unobtrusive measures in organizational theory: A reminder. *Administrative Science Quarterly, 24* (4), 650–659.
Weber, J., & Schaeffer, U. (2016). *Introduction to controlling* (15th ed., in German). Stuttgart, Germany: Schaeffer-Poeschel Verlag, 280–295.
Webster, J. & Watson, R.T. (2002): Analyzing the past to prepare for the future: Writing a literature review. MIS Quarterly, 26 (2), xiii–xxiii (11 pages).

Weichel, P. & Herrmann, J. (2016): *Wie Controller von Big Data profitieren können*, Controlling & Management Review Special Edition 1-2016. CMR-Sonderhefte. Springer Gabler, Wiesbaden, 8–14.

Wiegmann, L., Tretbar, T., & Strauß, E. (2014). Business partner 2.0. *Controlling, 26* (3), 197–201.

Willson, J. D., Bragg, S. M., & Roehl-Anderson, J. M. (2003). *Controllership, the work of the managerial accountant* (7th ed.). New York: John Wiley & Sons.

World Economic Forum. (2016). Shaping the future of digital economy and society. *World Economic Forum*. Retrieved from https://www.weforum.org/system-initiatives/the-digital-economy-and-society.

Yin, R. K. (2002). *Case study research: Design and methods* (4th ed.). London: Sage.

Yin, R. K. (2014). *Case study research: Design and methods* (5th ed.). Thousand Oaks, CA: Sage.

The manufacturer's authorised representative in the EU is Springer Nature Customer Service Centre GmbH, Europaplatz 3, 69115 Heidelberg, Germany. If you have any concerns regarding our products, please contact ProductSafety@springernature.com

Printed and bound by CPI Group (UK) Ltd, Croydon, CR0 4YY
02/10/2026
02226898-0002